FRIEND REQUEST ACCEPTED

CONNECTING IN A DISCONNECTED WORLD

ANDREW MACHOTA | CEO NEW TOWN CONNECTIONS

MRA
MEDIA GROUP

Friend Request Accepted

Connecting In A Disconnected World

by Andrew Machota

Copyright © 2017 by MRA Media Group

ISBN 978-0-9992489-0-4

www.NewTownConnections.com

CONTENTS

ACKNOWLEDGEMENTS

I'd like to thank my parents first and foremost for giving me the tools to write this book and for always believing in me. Without them, this book wouldn't exist. I'm sure my mom, an elementary school teacher for 40 years, is still having a good laugh that her son who never really was interested in reading and writing as a kid ended up writing a book. I'd also like to thank all my friends for the continuous encouragement to make this happen as well.

A very big shout out to my alma mater, Indiana University, for without my experiences there and my time spent studying abroad, I wouldn't be here today either. I could have just gone through the motion and been any other alumni, but it was my time spent in the Kelley School of Business where it all came together during those four formidable years in Bloomington, Indiana. Hoosier Hospitality is alive and well.

Thanks to Steve Gianfilippo, Founder of Station House St. Pete and Denny Gallagher, Owner of Dominion Payroll Services of Florida for providing me the space and environment to write this book over many weekends.

I'm very grateful for many things every day and for the 'chance' meetings I've had throughout my life that have led me to where I am today. Remember friends, there really are no such things as 'chance' meetings. Everything you do is a sign that is meant to lead you in the right direction – it's up to you to pay attention so you can follow your own life path. If you believe in yourself and that good things will come your way, they will. Keep moving forward and chase your dreams. If a farm town guy from Indiana can do what I have done, then why not you?

INTRODUCTION

Welcome to my world! I'm Andrew and I hail from a small town in Indiana called Rolling Prairie. I'm proud of where I'm from but I can sure tell you one thing: I'm never going back. One year ago, I never would have imagined I would be where I am today, let alone thirty years ago when I was growing up in that farm town. But I believe in destiny—a personal path laid out for each of us, that is left up to us to follow. My path led me to my purpose: helping people form genuine friendships in a society that has become increasingly disconnected.

For thousands of years, human beings have had to meet people in real life, to start conversations in person and determine who their friends are from there. Only in the last fifteen years did people start to shift away from meeting people in person to meeting people online. The popularity of social media and other online platforms doesn't change the innate desire we all have as humans to have real relationships, real friendships, and real conversations. If given the choice, most people would rather meet people in real life versus online or through a mobile app;

it's much easier to gauge a person's character first-hand than through a digital device.

In today's age of digital technology where people think they're more connected to each other, I would argue that the exact opposite is true. We are all more disconnected because technology gets between us. Texting is the default when you want to get in touch with someone. The art of conversation has gone by the wayside. Having 1,000 "friends" on Facebook or 2,000 "connections" on LinkedIn means little when it comes to real-life relationships. Building meaningful relationships still remains an in-person skill to have.

Searching for a future wife or husband should not follow the same process as browsing for a pair of jeans on Amazon.com—but that's where our culture has shifted to, with mobile apps and websites. It's easy to browse faces online and say, "She's beautiful, smart, funny, charming," and so on... but none of those qualities mean you would have actual chemistry with that person. Real chemistry is determined in person; sparks can't fly through a smartphone or a website.

The same concept applies to friendships. However, it's socially awkward to go up to someone at a bar and say "Hi, I'm Andrew, want to be friends?" Unfortunately, people would think you're weird. No comment on whether or not I've actually tried that line at a bar! This book presents new avenues for building real relationships and making real friends—friends you trust, friends you can rely on, friends you have something in common with—while eliminating as much of the social awkwardness as possible.

Aside from exploring different ways to make friends as an adult, this book also takes a different approach by discussing how to find yourself throughout that process. I know I've changed a lot from the time I was twenty-two years old to thirty-two years old and beyond. It's part of life. Friends come and go based on where we are at in our own lives; people get married, have kids, move away, and change. Friends you thought were your good friends turn out to be fair-weather friends, and friends you thought were just acquaintances can come through in the clutch.

NEW TOWN CONNECTIONS

To address the challenges of making new friends that are relevant to your current stage of adult life, I started my own company called New Town Connections. It is a social club for young professionals who are looking to meet other like-minded people in a fun, social, and welcoming environment.

I've moved to new cities multiple times and the process to go about making new friends is difficult, to say the least. I've also lived, worked and studied abroad, which actually served as the key impetus for starting New Town Connections, due to my own experiences of feeling isolated, lonely and depressed.

When I was twenty years old, I left the small town behind to spend six months studying abroad in England. I never really felt welcomed or accepted while in Europe and when I came back to the US, I vowed that I would do my best to ensure that no one else I met ever felt the same way I did when I lived abroad.

However, I happened to have the same experience of isolation again, this time in my own country. When I left college, I moved to Indianapolis for my first job and ran into the same issue as before. I was new in town, didn't know anyone, felt isolated and had no clue where to meet people or what to do. One would think that it would be easy to make friends in that city because I'm from Indiana. But the exact opposite was true. I grew up three hours north of Indianapolis and yet I found it hard to identify with others; I felt I was on my own island going to work, playing tennis, and trying to meet people without any help. It was tough. I lived there for eight years and yet only had a handful of friends after that time, because I never figured out where I could go to make true friends.

Only after my most recent move to Florida did I figure out how to make genuine, real-life friends as an adult. I had to step out of my comfort zone and establish my own footprint. It was difficult, but it forced me to become who I was meant to be. I had all these gifts that were deep inside me sitting dormant while I was in Indiana—my gifts of endless amounts of energy, the ability to remember people's names, to connect people, and be a master event coordinator all came to light when I moved to Florida.

I had an "aha moment" when I realized I was born to start New Town Connections and help other people make friends. All of my previous challenges and experiences led me to where I am today—to writing this book, to running events, to being a man about town. I hope you get something out of this book that you choose to apply in your own quest for new friendships.

Keep in mind, it's one thing to read a book, but it's another to take action. In order to make it easy for you to make real progress, I have broken this guide down into 18 steps. Don't just be a bystander – be an active participant in your life. These steps will help you break through some of the mental blocks that have kept you stuck—they will help you to put down your phone, turn off the TV and get out there!

Chapter 1

THE TWO MOST IMPORTANT QUESTIONS

Do you care?

Can I trust you?

Who would have known that those two questions—posed to me at the age of fourteen by my high school baseball coach—would have such a profound impact on my life? What did I know about life at fourteen? I was more concerned with impressing my high school peers, looking cool, and talking to girls. But for some reason, those two questions stuck with me. The more I thought about them, the more I realized they were the fabric of every solid friendship I'd ever had.

Have you ever had a friend or significant other who didn't care about you or didn't trust you? If so, the odds are that the relationship didn't work out very well, right? You can't be good friends if you don't care about each other and trust each other. These two "simple" yet complex traits go hand in hand.

In the age of digital technology, it has become harder and harder to trust people. Just because information is readily available online, doesn't mean it is creditworthy. On the contrary, technology makes it much more difficult to weed out who is real versus who is fake, since it is quite easy to sit behind a computer and lie about various things. Even in person, I can stand before you all day long and spew out words, but if my actions aren't in alignment with what I'm saying, then they're just words. You cannot succumb to believing everything people say.

In today's era, we have to take a new approach in order to determine the answers to these two all-important questions. After years of struggling as an adult to make quality friends, I now apply a few tests to everyone I meet to determine if they have what it takes to form a genuine, meaningful friendship. My simple system of tests has led me to my own inner circle of trust to the tune of ten people. This circle is fluid, in that new people come and go every year. Some friends burn out, some prove they are just acquaintances, and some new friends show up unexpectedly.

Just like a job application, I vet my inner circle thoroughly through actions more so than words. These are people I've predominantly known for more than a couple of years who have proven they care and are trustworthy.

HOW TO KNOW IF SOMEONE CARES

If you want to see if someone truly cares, give them a small task to do. Maybe it's asking him or her to pick you up from work one day to go to a happy hour, or asking for help when it comes to planning a birthday celebration. It doesn't have to be a big test; just ask for help and see who comes through.

When I meet people at a networking event, I always like to ask how I can help them. If they ask how they can help me in return, there's a good chance that they care. Another thing you can do is ask people a question that usually requires them to ask the same question back to you. The easiest: "Where are you from?" Seems simple enough: "I'm from Indiana, where are you from?" It's natural for someone to ask that question right back.

Ask two or three similar questions to see if there's any response back, such as "How long you have you lived here?" Or, "What type of work are you involved in?" If I start asking these kinds of questions and people don't ask me anything in return, red flags start going off in my head; usually, it's all downhill from there. After three such questions, if a person is disengaged, then exit from there. Time is valuable; don't spend it talking to people who have no interest in getting to know you.

Another way to gauge if someone cares is if he or she goes above and beyond to include you—in a conversation or event. One time while working abroad in Dubai, my co-worker Suhaib asked what I was doing for the weekend. I told him I had nothing planned, to which he replied, "Alright my friend, let's take a road trip to Abu Dhabi." And off we went. He went out of his way to take me out because he knew it was no fun being in a foreign country without any friends. That was how I knew he cared. He made an extra effort that no one else did.

THE TRUSTWORTHY TEST

I define trust as knowing someone has your back, through the good times and the bad times. Of course, it is a two-way street. Trust has to be reciprocal. You cannot expect others to have your back if you don't have theirs; one-sided relationships eventually implode as one person will feel slighted over time. Here are five steps I take to determine if someone is trustworthy—that are good to hold yourself up against, as well.

1) TRUST YOUR GUT

"When you know, you know." Let me guess—you've heard that statement at least 1,000 times from your friends when you ask the story of how Jack and Jill met. "Oh yes, when I met Jill, we just knew. It was love at first sight." And then you probably rolled your eyes. But maybe there is some truth to that statement—your gut knows things. Your head says one thing, your heart says another, but it's your gut that gives you the real advice. Do you remember a time when you second-guessed yourself and said, "Damn it, I should have trusted my gut?" I sure do. We tend to over think things. If your gut tells you something, stick to it.

When you're talking to someone new, what's your initial feeling? Good, bad, neutral? I asked myself that question when I considered if I should trust Suhaib. He was my co-worker, so I wasn't concerned that I would disappear into the desert and not come back. But I did make a gut check.

Whether you're living or studying abroad or you just moved to a new city, you will have to rely on your gut more than usual—more than your head and your heart, because again, in the modern world, who can you really trust? But the truth is, sometimes you just have to take a risk. Venture on the side of safety first, but in the end, you might just have to trust someone enough to say, "Screw it, let's go take a trip to Abu Dhabi and see what happens!" That is how a life gets lived—and how you find out if, when push comes to shove, you can really trust someone.

2) GIVE IT TIME

A person's true character is revealed over time; through words, actions, inaction and general accountability, you will be able to determine one's character. Just like with a job, a person may shine bright like a diamond the first six months, but then after a year or two that shine fades away.

For friends to establish trust, it takes time. When you see how someone new interacts in certain situations and how he or she treats other people, you get a good gauge as to who this person really is. If I see someone treat others with disrespect, or in a way that I would not want to be treated, then I know that person is not someone I want as a friend.

You have to be careful with who you trust. Hold onto information carefully and be leery of people you've only known a short period of time. Give them a year or two to establish themselves and prove their character, before you become complete and total BFF's.

And don't forget, you have to prove to your friends that you are trustworthy, too. If someone gives you a secret and tells you not to say anything, you best keep that secret to yourself. If not, your credibility will diminish in a matter of seconds and you will find it extremely difficult to get it back. As the old saying goes – your reputation takes years to build but if you make one mistake, it can evaporate overnight.

3) OWN IT

We all make mistakes, say dumb things, and regret the words that come out of our mouth from time to time. Occasionally, being human, we get in the heat of the moment and shoot from the hip. No one is perfect; people are complex and generally hard to understand. What is important is that we own up to our mistakes.

There have definitely been times when I said something to a friend I shouldn't have, and word eventually came back around. We're only as good as our word, and if we end up lying about what we said or did, our credibility only diminishes further.

People will respect you much more for owning a mistake, apologizing, and moving on—just like you will respect someone else who does the same.

If you make a mistake, figure out what happened and why, and then make sure you don't do that again. In turn, you should expect the same from people you call your friends.

4) GET REAL

If you want to determine whether or not someone can be trusted, you need to engage with them in a real conversation that is not surface level.

I define surface-level conversations as topics related to weather, sports, topical information, current events, and anything else with little substance. Real conversations involve who you are, what you want to accomplish, where you're going in life, your passions, your desires, and the pursuit of happiness. These topics offer a deeper level of conversation than what occurs in a typical group setting or at an event. These are the kinds of conversations that take place one-on-one.

We all know that while at a football game, the conversation will be more topical and light versus having a private conversation at a wine bar with a friend. The art of a one-on-one conversation is opening up, and getting down to topics that require thought and discussion. And always remember, one-on-one conversations are two-way streets. You have to let the other person share their point of view, what drives him or her, and so on; this practice will keep the conversation lively and fresh. Have you ever sat in a conversation where one person did all the talking and you were left nodding your head saying, "Yes, uh-huh," for the majority of the conversation? I call those conversations a waste of time and not the kind that happen among real friends.

5) REGULARLY GET TOGETHER

Being a good friend requires consistent engagement. Both parties need to commit to getting together regularly at times that are convenient for each other. If one-on-ones happen only once every six months, that's not the sign of a quality friendship. How can you be a real friend if you can't even make time to spend two hours a month to have a conversation? Using the excuse "too busy" is the biggest cop-out for any relationship. We're all busy. If one-on-ones don't happen regularly, your "friend" is probably more of an acquaintance.

Consistency is the key to communication with friends and the more you stay in touch, the more of a relationship you'll build— and the more opportunities you'll have to build trust.

6) STAY ENGAGED

When you are speaking with new people, notice their level of interest in what you are saying. Are they engaging in positive body language? Do they lean in to listen? Are they positioned in front of you or to the side of you? Are they making eye contact? Are they checking their phone while you're talking? Are they asking questions that relate to the topic you're discussing?

If a person isn't paying attention and seems aloof, that's because they are. Know that it's ok to exit such a conversation abruptly. Say something to the effect of, "It was so nice to meet you Jim, but I have to say hi to some friends who just got here. Have a great night!" Shake Jim's hand and off you go into the sunset. If someone can't be considerate or engaging in conversation, then save yourself some time and move onto someone else who can.

WORDS OF CAUTION

At times you may be tempted to remain friends with someone who doesn't demonstrate that they really care, or who does not pass the trustworthy test. But here's a word of advice:

It is better to be alone than to be with people who you think are your friends but who really aren't. I think we've all seen enough movies to know what that is like: The popular kids pretend to befriend someone smart so they can copy his answers on a test. After they use that person, they no longer are friends and the straight A student feels duped. Like I said—trust takes time. Making friends fast is easy; if you're looking for good friends, weed out those who don't treat you right.

You may fear burning bridges or hurting someone else's feelings, but here's another important tip:

You need to stop caring about what others think or say. I know this is easier said than done, but it is better to live a life in your own shoes than to try to be friends with everyone. Conforming to who others want you to be will make you fit in with them, whether that's by what you wear, what you say, how you say things or any number of other items. But changing who you are to join a group or be "friends" with someone will only last so long; sooner or later you'll revert to who you really are. So, DON'T DO IT! Find a person or a group that fits your personality. Stand up for yourself and who you are.

No matter your skin color, religion, political affiliation, your upbringing, your status, your job, or your sexuality...we all shine in our own unique ways. Don't let anyone tell you otherwise. Haters will always hate because that's what they do, but you can't let them get to you. Smile, wave, and keep on being you.

Finally, **Know your acquaintances from your friends.** Acquaintances are people who come and go through your life at various stages just like a warm summer breeze. It's your choice how you want to treat acquaintances, but know them apart from your friends; it can become quite tricky if the two become intermixed and you're left figuring out who is who.

TAKEAWAYS:

- A real friend steps up when you need them. Give people a simple task or two to see if they really care. If not, then move on.

- Trust has to be earned (and you have to earn it, too!)

- Spend one-on-one time consistently with good friends. Build a rapport. Lasting friendships take time and effort.

Chapter 2

EVERY PERSON YOU MEET MATTERS

Have you ever wondered why certain people entered and exited your life during particular times? Was it pure coincidence that they came into your life when you needed them and left when you didn't? The universe works in magical ways. I never expected to find myself in Florida, writing a book about making friends. But here I am, because of a number of people who entered my life at particular times.

In 2010, I attended a tennis tournament in Cincinnati. There, I met a photographer who lived in Tampa. He told me I should come check the city out; we could play tennis and I'd get to visit a place I'd never been. Being a yes man, I said, "Sure!" Once I visited, I knew the city was the place I belonged; it was a calling. A few months later, I packed up my belongings and made the move. Is it crazy to make a leap into the unknown? A little. But if you believe that what you're doing is right, then no, it's not that big of a leap. At least that's how I felt.

I knew the life I had been living wasn't right for me. I was born and raised in Indiana, went to Indiana University, was recruited from there to work at a CPA firm in Indianapolis, and that was my life. I'm happiest when I have the opportunity to be outside playing under the sun. I didn't get much of a chance to do that in Indiana. So I figured, why should I have to wait to retire before moving to Florida? I departed for greener pastures to the south and never looked back.

I think a lot of people get stuck in a rut after college; they do what's been done for years—go to high school, then college, find a job, get married, have kids, become grandparents, then die. If you're happy with that lifestyle, by all means, follow that path. But if you're not happy where you're living, or with your job, your career, or where your life is going... then make a change! What are you waiting for? The longer you stay in a situation that doesn't make you happy, the harder it will be to escape.

Just because you're born somewhere doesn't mean you have to stay there. Moving to Florida was the best decision I have made in my entire life. Moving to a new city takes you out of your comfort zone. You have to adapt, fight, and find your way to survive. But that's what's fun, right? Well, at least it was for me because I always like a good adventure into the unknown.

In any case, I always think to myself, what if I didn't meet that guy at the tennis tournament? Would I have ever moved to Florida? I don't know, but possibly not. That's where my belief in destiny comes into play—the idea that you have to keep your eyes and ears open and be aware of what's going on around you. If I had said no, I'll pass on visiting Florida, then I wouldn't be writing this book today, that's for sure. I'd probably still be pushing papers as a CPA back in Indiana, living a completely different life.

Instead, it took me a few years to get settled into my new city, during which time I figured out what I was meant to be doing. I found my true calling: helping others to meet people and build quality friendships. From there, my life started really coming together—all because I met that one person in Cincinnati.

THE NETWORKING CIRCUIT

When I first moved to Tampa over six years ago, I only knew a handful of people. I didn't know where to start in regards to making friends. I tried several outlets before finally joining the networking circuit. First, I joined some tennis leagues and made a few older guy friends (note to self: it's tough to be good friends with people fifteen years older as they generally are in a different stage of life). Then I joined some volleyball leagues, then my alumni association, and then salsa dancing.

The networking circuit was the one place that I could meet a number of people very quickly and expand my own circle of influence in a matter of weeks, versus months or years via other activities. However, you meet so many people when you go to networking events that it's hard to vet who's a "good" contact and who is not. In addition, most people all ask the same question: "What do you do?" After a while, you tend to burn out because you see the same sales people at the same events pitching whatever they're trying to sell. These challenges helped give me the idea to create and launch New Town Connections, as I thought to myself there had to be a better way to meet new people other than going to networking events five nights a week.

Going to networking events can be a bit awkward. Everyone is standing around wearing name tags and you have to force yourself to go talk to new people. If you're a female, you'll probably have a bunch of random guys come talk to you—not to become your friend or talk business with you, but to hit on you. For these reasons, the word "networking" tends to have a negative connotation, and often people only associate it with business people.

But what about all the other professions that aren't in the business field? Surely there needs to be a way for those people to get out and meet people, too. Imagine all the doctors, nurses, teachers, air force pilots, engineers, scientists, and so on who would like to meet people. At New Town Connections, we bring everyone together regardless of what they do and give people introductions to help facilitate conversations. We also take the time to interview and vet all potential members, which helps eliminate some of the risk of being approached at an event by people who make you uncomfortable.

RIGHT PLACE, RIGHT TIME

Once I joined the networking circuit, everything in my life began to fall in place. More and more people serendipitously entered my life. I began asking myself about everyone I met, "Why did I meet this person?" It wasn't about how I could use this person for my own gain, rather it was more of a thought process. If I could figure out why we met, then I could make a better assessment of this person's role in my life and fully understand what I was meant to learn from this person, or offer to this person.

Not everyone we meet is meant to have a significant level of importance in our lives. Some people stay in our lives forever, and others for only a very short period of time. But no matter how long they're in our lives, we met for a definite reason. Sometimes you'll know the reason in a matter of minutes, sometimes it will take more time.

I like to tell the story of why I met my friend Natalie. I was out with my best friend Tracee one night at a bar when I tapped a random girl (Natalie) to take a picture of us. She politely obliged and noticed that my phone cover was of my alma mater—Indiana University. She asked if I was from there and I said, "You bet." Randomly enough, she too was from Indiana. We exchanged information and

I told her we should hang out sometime. I also told her that I could help her with job hunting, as we both worked in the same field. We kept in touch and she took me up on that offer.

Natalie had a vision of working in Miami to be closer to her family. I put her in touch with my colleague in Miami who helped her land a new job there. And just like that, she was off to Miami. If you put yourself in the right place at the right time, good things happen. I could have easily picked any other girl to take a picture, but for some reason I picked Natalie.

But how do you know if it's the right time or place? You don't always—but if you stay home all day every day, I guarantee you that's not the right time or place to meet anyone.

Here's another story. My friend Kyle and I met at an alumni function. He was looking for a job so he could plant some roots in Florida. Fortunately, he met a woman from our college who was able to help secure him a job. Through that job, he was able to meet his now wife. All that transpired from going to an alumni networking event? Sounds crazy, but it's what happens when you take that step and walk through the front door of any place, any event, or any outing.

It takes an effort to put yourself out there, and it takes that secondary effort to connect with people and understand why they're in your life. If you can figure out the latter, you'll be light years ahead of other people who never truly grasp why certain people are in their lives—and why certain negative people keep on hanging around.

Here's a tip: It's up to you to purge the negative people from your life—they're going to stick around because you have yet to learn how to give them the boot. They came into your life for a reason, remember? Everyone has a lesson to teach us. Learn the lesson, then cast them away if they're a negative presence in your life.

BELIEVE AND YOU WILL ACHIEVE

When I started my company, New Town Connections, I wanted to develop a diverse team of people from all walks of life and industries. And before I knew it, it happened. I was able to meet a number of people and build a team of women and men from different parts of the world, who spoke multiple languages and who were raised in different cultures, to form this amazing team. These situations happen all the time in my life, which is how I came to believe that every person we meet matters. It's just up to us to decide what we do with these relationships.

I know that most people I meet out networking or at events will fall by the wayside; it's nearly impossible to keep track of all the people I meet week in and week out. But it's an interesting challenge to see who sticks, and who will impact my life. You might be thinking, "How do I know if the person I met last night will impact my life? Is there a way to tell?" Unfortunately, no, there's not an easy way. You just have to start conversations and see where things go from there. In fact, you may meet someone today who impacts your life five years from now. You never know.

TAKEAWAYS:

- If you're not happy where you're living, or with your job, your career, or where your life is going... then make a change! The longer you stay in a situation that doesn't make you happy, the harder it will be to escape.

- When you meet someone new, ask yourself: Why did I meet this person? They're in your life for a reason.

- To be in the right place at the right time, you have to put yourself out there.

Chapter 3

FRAMEWORK FOR MAKING FRIENDS

Are you ready to begin the journey to making new friends? It all starts with one step. Whether that's walking through the front door of an event, signing up for an intramural sports team, joining a book club, or any other variety of activities...you have to put yourself out there. It's not easy, but it is a necessary fact if you want to have the social life you dream of. You can't make new friends from your living room couch. So, let's go! Grab your best pair of shoes because this journey is more than a quick walk to your neighborhood market.

In this book I've outlined 18 steps to guide you on your way; they are listed below and gone into much greater detail in the following chapters. Unfortunately, I can't be your wingman everywhere you go, however, my goal is for these steps to serve as your toolkit as you build your new social network. These are all critical steps to finding success meeting new people and making new friends—trust me, I've learned the hard way.

STEP 1: FIND YOUR HAPPINESS FIRST

You are a reflection of how you feel, and people can see that immediately. As such, if you want to attract other people to be friends with who are happy, you have to be happy. This is the most important of all the steps, which is why it is first. In this section, I'll guide you on how to take control of your own happiness.

STEP 2: ADJUST YOUR MINDSET - THE POWER OF POSITIVITY

Why do bad things happen to good people? Why are some people stuck in the rut of negativity? We'll explore how to look at things in a different light in this section—how to focus on all the positives that surround our lives every day, versus worrying about things outside of our control. When you bring positive energy to a room full of people, you will soon become a magnet for other people who can feel your energy and who will want to be around you.

STEP 3: IT'S TIME TO GET OUT THERE

The hardest part about making new friends is putting yourself out there. We've all been there, myself included. No one wants to walk into a room full of strangers and not know what to say or what to do. It's awkward and uncomfortable. But, we have to start somewhere so take that deep breath and go for it! This section will discuss different techniques for getting out there so you'll have the confidence to be able to own the room.

STEP 4: KNOW BEFORE YOU GO

Would you show up to a final exam without studying at all? If not, then why would you attend an event without knowing a little about what's going on and what you're getting yourself into? This chapter will teach you how to manage your time and experience by planning in advance.

STEP 5: MASTER THE INTRODUCTION

What's your go-to question when you first meet someone? Do you have something ready to go in an instant? Life favors those who are prepared. I will share my tips on how to think on your feet, ask engaging questions, and really listen. You only get one shot to impress someone with your verbal skills and in this section, I'll help you to know what to say at the right time and right place.

STEP 6: MANAGE THE NON-VERBALS

Managing non-verbal communication is just as important, if not more important, than understanding and reacting to verbal communication. People often misinterpret body language, or just don't read it at all, as most of us have never had formal training on how to pick up on non-verbal cues. Being able to hone in on subtleties and be a master of non-verbal communication will put you far above others when it comes to making new friends.

STEP 7: FOLLOW UP / FOLLOW THROUGH

It's pretty easy to become forgettable today. With all the distractions in our lives, we have to take a few more steps than we used to in order to grab people's attention. Here we'll go over why it's important to follow up with people and what is the best methodology for following through on your word. To ensure that you do not become forgettable, you have to stand out from the crowd, and following up and following through are two of the best practices to accomplish that goal.

STEP 8: ACTIONS SPEAK LOUDER THAN WORDS

In the digital age we live in, you must discern between who talks without backing up their words and who follows through on what they said they were going to do. It's easy to say one thing today on social media then forget about it tomorrow. However, you leave a digital footprint and your reputation is at stake for things you say even if you do forget about them. This chapter discusses how to monitor what you say and ensure your words match your actions.

STEP 9: BE REAL, BE GENUINE, BE YOURSELF

The biggest determining factor of making friends today is being genuine. I can't recall ever hearing about anyone who likes to be around fake people. Your creditability and likability will go much further if you stay true to yourself and don't try to be something you're not. There's something to be said about being authentic today, and here we'll talk about different ways to bring out your personality and really be you.

STEP 10: STEP OUTSIDE YOUR COMFORT ZONE

In order to make new friends, you have to expand your horizons and start doing things out of your comfort zone. Here I'll talk about two of my favorite ways to step outside one's comfort zone—dancing, and traveling abroad!

STEP 11: TEAM NO SLEEP

This has been my go-to mantra for several years now, along with "can't stop won't stop." This may not be an official team, but

I would love for you to join me on the adventure of a lifetime. The more you go out, the more people you meet, the more invitations you'll receive, and the more friends you'll make. The "team" does require a significant amount of energy, however this chapter will discuss how the only barrier to joining the team is your mindset.

STEP 12: JUST SAY "YES"

The easiest way to meet a large number of people in a short amount of time is to just say "yes" to every invitation you get. In this chapter I'll talk about the mindset required to be a "yes" man or a "yes" woman—but I'll also share some tips about when it can be best to say no.

STEP 13: CHANGE YOUR ROUTINES

Rules were made to be broken. The same can be said about routines. It's nice to follow certain day-to-day routines, but overall, routines are boring and you don't want to get stuck in that rut of doing the same thing over and over or else you'll eventually burn out. This section offers tips on how to keep things fresh.

STEP 14: FIND YOUR PURPOSE, FOLLOW YOUR PASSION

Much is said about passion, but what about your purpose? Why are you here and what are your gifts? And what does this have to do with making friends? As Mark Twain said best: "The two most important days in your life are the day you are born and the day you find out why." What is your why? We'll do a deep dive here to help you to see where your purpose lies and how that can lead to new and meaningful friendships.

STEP 15: TREAT OTHERS LIKE YOU'D LIKE TO BE TREATED

All good friendships are a two-way street and how you treat others will come back to you tenfold. If you want to be treated a certain way by your friends, you must set the tone from your side and treat people with respect. Here I'll talk about what is required to stand out as a great friend, and how to be a team player.

STEP 16: LOVE IS ALL YOU NEED

Who says that loving others is hard? It sure doesn't have to be. In fact, it should be relatively easy. That doesn't mean you need to go around saying, "I love you" to everyone, however there's nothing wrong with telling people how you feel about them and bringing the love with you wherever you go. People can feel it, and love truly does become contagious. Here I'll offer tips on how you can let your love shine and let others know where you stand in your friendship.

STEP 17: NO EXCUSES

Too often we make excuses for anything and everything: I'm too busy. I'm too tired. I can't do it. I'll try to be there. To be a good friend you must hold yourself accountable and get away from all the tired excuses that have been overused. This chapter focuses on how to take initiative and get out of your own way.

STEP 18: JUST BE...

This final step is all about "how" you need to be in order to be a great friend—starting with being present. You can't make new friends if you're playing on your phone when you're together with them! Here are some tips about being engaging, humble, genuinely interested, and FEARLESS.

So what do you say? Ready to get started? Let's take the first step...

Chapter 4

STEP ONE: FIND YOUR HAPPINESS FIRST

This book takes a different approach to making friends as an adult by exploring how to find yourself in the process. To me, this is a very important step to building real friendships. How can you know what to look for in someone else, if you don't even understand who you are? How can you attract people into your life when the energy you send out is negative? Like attracts like. We assume you want to attract happy people into your life, so let's first focus on how you can increase your own state of happiness.

HAPPINESS DEFINED

What is happiness? Is it a state of mind? Is it something tangible? Can you feel it? Can you touch it? Is there a formula that can be used to determine how to make you happy?

Happiness can be found anywhere—you just have to look for it. It's in you, me, and everyone else. Since no two people are alike, there is no single definition or path to happiness. That's the great thing about it—it's different for everyone.

My happiness is based on the experiences I've had, and the new ones I look forward to. It's also about the people in my life. I could care less about any material items – for me those are meaningless. I drive a Mazda, live in a quaint apartment and wear regular clothes from your typical men's stores from the mall. Does money buy happiness? Maybe for some people. For me, happiness comes from seeing the joy in others. When I open myself up and give more than I take, I feel happy. The old saying, "it's better to give than to receive" holds very true to me.

So what makes you happy? Think about it and write it down. Is it traveling? Watching movies? Hanging out with friends? Reading? Painting? Working out? Again, there are a million different things that make people happy. You need to focus on what makes *you* happy and forget about what happiness means to others. There's no need to worry about what other people have. If they want to drive a fancy car or live in a big house, more power to them. In the age of technology and social media, it's too easy to compare your life to others. Don't do it! Focus only on what makes *you* happy—the things on your list.

TAKE CONTROL OF YOUR HAPPINESS

It is hard work to make new friends. It takes a lot of time, and definitely a lot of energy to put yourself out there in the beginning. But it's worth it! Everyone wants friends to talk to, to hang out with, to share life with through experiences. I like to travel around the world by myself, but I'm never truly alone because I enjoy staying in hostels and meeting up with people there. We are social by nature, and we all need other people in our lives.

I find my happiness by meeting as many people as I can on a day-to-day to basis. What's your daily activity that makes you happy? Think about it. What's one thing you can do every single day that makes you happy? Got it? Write it down and then start doing it. Being happy really doesn't have to be so difficult. There's plenty to do regardless of which city or town you live in. If you live in a small town, then create things to do.

My farm town back in Indiana was a booming metropolis of 500 people; you can imagine the things I had to entertain myself growing up. I had a ton of energy, no technology, no cable TV (until I was in high school) – what did I do to have fun? I stayed outside and played as often as I could. Whether it was climbing trees, shooting hoops, riding my bike or anything else. I found things to do—you have to, or else you'll just be bored out of your mind watching TV, Netflix, or trolling social media feeds. Figure out what makes you happy and do it. And if there isn't an opportunity to do what makes you happy where you live, create it! I'm sure that's not always applicable, but do the best you can. Opportunities are out there.

When I was living in Indiana, I was living as a shell of who I really am. I was living in the box that was bestowed upon me because I didn't know any better. I thought there was only one way to live life and that I had to conform to that. Part of my mission in this book is to encourage and enlighten you that there are thousands of ways to live your life. You just need to figure out what's best for you.

At the end of the day, your level of happiness lies in your own hands. You control your destiny. We all have decisions and choices to make every day; it's really an endless endeavor: What to eat for breakfast, what to wear for work, who to hang out with at night, what TV show to watch. It never ends. But your choice in friends plays a significant role in how happy you are. Be careful when you find yourself around negative people, because misery truly does love company. Don't fall into that trap. Find good friends and you will find happiness.

I like to think of happiness in terms of memories. It's always nice to look back on photographs and reminisce about the good times; doing so makes me happy. Life experiences, travels, people I met, stories from the past. You can't put a price tag on those memories. Being with people who lift you up, inspire you, encourage you, who share the same beliefs—those are the people you want in your life. Those are the people who will help you in your quest for happiness.

There are plenty of studies out there that suggest having real, solid friendships and social connections help with not just your general state of happiness but also with health and longevity. The longer you stay connected to your friends, the longer the life you'll most likely live. Having real friends over time truly is invaluable.

I feel blessed to be living the life I live every single day, and I hope you feel the same way. If not, take some time to meditate and be grateful for what you have, rather than what you don't have. If you're constantly wishing you had trendier items, a bigger car or a mansion, I strongly suggest you take a trip to any third-world country to humble yourself. When you see what other people live through on a day-to-day basis, the trivial items you don't have will become just that—trivial.

Once you get past a certain age in life you'll realize that the most important person in your life is you. Act like you want to act. Dress how you want to dress. Eat what you want to eat. Live the life you want to live. That's the best advice I can give you about finding your own happiness. Following your own path will help you shine in your own way—and help you attract the people into your life that will become your new best friends.

TAKEAWAYS:

- Block out all the noise and do what makes you happy—if an activity you love doesn't exist in your town, start it!

- Don't compare your life to others—there are as many unique definitions of happiness as there are people.

- Find the daily activity that makes you happy and do it.

Chapter 5

STEP TWO: ADJUST YOUR MINDSET - THE POWER OF POSITIVITY

What impact does your happiness have on others? More than you can imagine! People like to surround themselves with people who are happy. There's something about people smiling, laughing, and having fun. Other people want that feeling, too!

What does it take to be a positive person? Does it come naturally? Or can you shift your thinking to that mentality? I don't think positivity is a given; I have good days and bad days just like everyone else. However, no matter how bad the situation, I always look for the bright side, because bad things happen to good people on a daily basis.

I'm sure you've questioned yourself at times, "Why me? Why did I get into an accident? Why did I get fired? Why did my significant other break up with me?" I love to ask "why," because it's a critical thinking question – it makes you dig deeper as to what's going on and helps you move on from whatever just happened. My challenge to you is to flip or spin every bad situation in your life into something positive.

Example: I just got into a car accident.
Alternate response: I'm glad I'm not severely injured.

Example: My girlfriend just broke up with me.
Alternate response: I guess that means my next girlfriend will be even better because this one couldn't handle my awesomeness.

If you focus on the positive, good things will happen—you will even begin to perceive something as positive that you used to think was negative.

For making friends, you really do need to be positive and project that kindred spirit. Your vibe attracts your tribe, therefore if you're negative, you're only going to be attracting other negative people. In the same sense, if you're positive you'll be attracting other positive people to you. I don't know about you, but I'd much rather hang out with positive people as they inspire me, lift me up, give me encouragement, and pull me out from the dumps when I'm having a bad day.

Negative people? Well, they'll just keep you down, make you feel bad, tell you that life is tough, and that bad things are just bound to happen. Just like in the movie *Field of Dreams*, "if you build it, they will come." If you believe in negative thoughts, they will come. Aim to be that happy, go-lucky person that other people are drawn to. You don't have to be the life of the party, but your smile and positivity will go a long way in helping you meet new friends.

LUCK IS IN YOUR MIND

Have you ever met a person who seems to have luck running through their veins? They have it all—the nice car, the big house, the perfect family, the dream job, and so on? Are they really that lucky...or did something else have a hand in it?

Wherever I go, I always believe the weather will be perfect. And do you know what? Nine times out of ten, it is. If you believe that something is going to happen, odds are that it will, whether good or bad. Some people believe in Murphy's Law, that whatever could go wrong will go wrong. If you change your thoughts and reverse that, watch what happens. What if you said, what could go right, will go right? If you believe it, you'll be surprised what happens.

To me, one's beliefs are the daily signals we put out to the world: The energy, the vibes, the daily rituals. Your beliefs have to be your entitlements—that whatever is coming your way is yours to begin with: A new job, a new car, a relationship...anything. If you envision something is going to happen, and truly believe it, watch what unfolds.

I believe in vision boards—the more you see who you want to be or where you want to be, the more you'll believe it. You must reinforce your thoughts daily with positive images of either the end result you desire, or how you're going to get there.

Jenilee is a good friend of mine, and one of the first people to tell me about using a vision board. She's a big believer in vision boards, as using one has affected her life on more than one occasion. When she was going through a divorce, her life was upside down and she needed to re-center herself and focus on what was important to her and where her life was going. So she created a vision board and made plans to travel to Hawaii, to move, to start a new job, and envisioned her daughter happy in this new life. Several months later, all of those visions came to be. Her life turned out to be exactly as she had envisioned.

CASE STUDY: JENILEE

In 2009 I hit rock bottom. I had separated from my husband and was back at my mom's house with my nearly four-year-old daughter. The marriage was irreversible and I was at the end of my rope with my health. Before my marriage came to an end, I was already studying metaphysics, the power of intention, the laws of vibration, and anything that would help me align back to my truest self. I read books by authors Wayne Dyer, Deepak Chopra, Louise Hay, Brian Weiss, Bruce Lipton, Carl Jung, Jerry and Esther Hicks, and Eckhart Tolle, and listened to India Arie songs.

In 2010 I decided to venture into the world of vision boards. I had studied very meticulously what it would take to create an intentional board to bring forth my manifestations. I sat down and meditated with my board and thought about the feelings I wanted to feel, by understanding the contrast of that. At the time, I didn't feel at home, I felt lost, I was sick on bed rest, I suffered from anxiety and fear, I didn't understand life and I just really wanted to go to Hawaii one day to visit Wayne Dyer (this was just an internal yearning).

In my board, I added a quote from Maya Angelou- "I long, as does every human being, to be at home wherever I find myself." I posted pictures of a home, a woman doing yoga, of Maui, healthy foods, a woman balancing love, life, career, etc., dollar signs, and very intentional words that would describe what I wanted to feel. There was a longing beyond superficiality, so I focused on intention and every day I worked on facing my fears like my life depended on it, against many odds.

In 2011, I had lost everything: my job, my health, and my daughter, who was temporarily living four hours away with her dad. I had nothing to my name but twenty dollars cash, a few of my personal belongings, and a car with a full tank of gas. I drove to where my daughter was (Tampa Bay) and decided to enroll in school. Many things went wrong before they went right. I ended up in college, working full-time, and with my own apartment. The right people showed up, and I actually traveled to Maui in 2012. My life took a complete turn; there is more in between, but every adversity I faced had its corresponding vision board.

Looking at the board allowed me to visually see what my purpose was, and to know what to focus on daily. Physically seeing everything I wanted to invite into my life through words and pictures actually invited those things in.

I have done vision boards for many years now, and every year the board changes as I grow with different intentions. I have even taught vision board workshops; I have manifested homes, jobs, relationships and even a car. However, the board is to keep me accountable for my inner work. I never met Wayne Dyer in physical form (perhaps because I didn't put it on the vision board!), but vision boards have been a great reminder as to why I wake up in the morning, and what has been and can still be possible for me.

EMPOWER OTHERS

What does it take to lift others up? All it takes to be inspirational and encouraging is your time and effort. However, the impact you make will be more profound than you can imagine— because most people don't make the effort. When was the last time that someone commented that you are awesome? Or that you did a great job? Or that you're doing something worthwhile in life? Probably a long time ago. Don't worry—you're in the same boat as 98% of everyone else. Very rarely do people go out of their way to say nice things other than the usual surface level conversations about your clothes, your style, your car, your house, etc.

I challenge you to look someone in the eye and say, "You are awesome. You have touched my life and a lot of other people's lives, just by being you. My life wouldn't be the same without you." That's it. Be prepared for some tears if it's someone you're close to and have never said anything like that to before. Words are very powerful and when you mean what you say, that genuine feeling shines through. Your friends won't forget what you said because you will touch them so deeply. The same can be said about being negative. If you say something that's mean-spirited and negative about a person, whether to their face or not, those words will affect them and they'll remember it. Choose to empower others with positivity.

Being nice doesn't cost anything. Make it a routine in your life to encourage others. Be a cheerleader. Pick people up when they're down. Everyone needs a hand occasionally. Don't be afraid to be the person that sticks your hand out to pull people up with you on your way to the top.

WORDS OF CAUTION

Avoid social media commentary. When you're having a bad day, don't post it, don't tweet it, don't let the world know about it. We see this behavior every day across all social media, but no one likes a complainer. In the busy lives we lead, there is little time to waste on the trivial things. Save your time, and either keep the problem to yourself or post a funny comment about the situation instead. The more you focus on the negative, the worse things get. And in contrast, the more you focus on the positive, the better things will get. It's all about perspective; don't lose sight of what's important to you. Stay on track and stay positive.

TAKEAWAYS:

- Always think of the positives in any situation.

- Envision the life you want, believe in it, and watch what unfolds.

- Empower other people by saying something thoughtful and positive about them.

Chapter 6

STEP THREE: IT'S TIME TO GET OUT THERE

"Life moves pretty fast. If you don't stop and look around once in a while, you could miss it."
- Ferris Bueller

Now, it's time to put yourself out there. But with so many options out there, perhaps your first question is, "Where do I even start?"

My first suggestion is to start doing things you like—that's the easiest strategy, so start there. If you like a certain sport, join a sports league. If you like reading books, find a book club. If you're into networking, find some networking events to attend. The whole premise is that by doing things you enjoy, you'll meet others who share the same interests—which makes making friends that much easier because you already have something in common.

On the flip side, it can also be great to try something you're not good at or unsure if you like. I really enjoy stretching myself in this way, because it makes my brain work a little harder. Mix it up and try something new; you will meet people you would never have met anywhere else in life. Try a dance class, join a travel group, volunteer. Try anything!

Walking through the door is the first step to meeting people, regardless of what you're getting yourself into. I know that first step is tough and sometimes awkward and uncomfortable. It may give you anxiety. But don't worry—almost everyone else feels the same. You can always start small. There is no need to go to an event with 100 people when you can go to one with twenty.

My friend Becca is a very social person. At least that's how she seems from the outside now. But when I first met her, she was socially nervous and anxious when it came to networking events. These events were outside of her comfort zone; she found it awkward to go up and talk to random people about business or anything else.

Fast forward to several months later. Becca practiced her social and conversational skills through events at New Town Connections, and now has all the confidence in the world to walk into a room and own it—all because she took that first step through the front door of that first event. She didn't change overnight, but she perfected the art of conversation over time and now can be seen at any event with a glow around her.

CASE STUDY: BECCA

Making friends as an adult isn't an easy thing to do. For me personally, I find that it's easy to meet people and introduce myself on a surface level, but to actually develop a friendship can be tough. Opening up isn't an easy task for someone like me.

New Town Connections helped make it easier, however, because it's a members based group with like-minded people. Over time, since you're going to the same events as other members, you actually get to know the people in the group. The best part is, you don't have to put forth the actual work of planning events to get your new friends all in one place.

Another friend of mine, Christina has a similar story. She moved to Florida from Maryland and was shy and unsure of herself prior to joining New Town Connections. Under the team's stewardship, she slowly but steadily built up her self-confidence at our events. She started to believe she could do whatever she wanted in her life because she now had a strong, positive support group backing her. She left her job in the medical field and went into sales and has become a very successful saleswoman. She told me that if it wasn't for joining the group, she would have returned home to Maryland because she felt so alone and isolated in Florida. It was her new, strong social network of friends that helped her become who she is today.

When I first moved to Florida I faced the same challenge of walking into the unknown. I like to do a variety of things, but I wasn't sure where to start. I Googled "club sports," as I figured that would be a good place to meet people who also played sports. I joined a beach volleyball league and began my foray into meeting people. Volleyball isn't something I was always into, but I had to adapt to where I moved to, step out of my comfort zone, and make the best of the situation.

From volleyball, I ventured into a number of other activities including salsa dancing, tennis, kickball, and networking. I like to tell people that there is an underestimated power in networking, which can be applied to almost anything. Everywhere you go, you're going to meet people. So every day, you have an opportunity to network, even if you don't really even think about it as networking.

"Networking" has such a negative, business connotation to it. But don't let that dissuade you! People advance their careers and personal lives through networking because it really is all about "who you know." The people in life who are the most successful also have the most established network of people. But how does one obtain that trusted, established, network of people? It takes time, unfortunately, as relationships aren't built overnight and it all starts with that first step of putting yourself out there.

Use the Internet as your tool; if you're interested in business networking in Topeka, Kansas, then Google "Young professionals Topeka Kansas" and see what groups show up. And if you're looking for a mixture of networking and socializing, then my company, New Town Connections may just happen to be there, and we would love for you to join us!

A NOTE ON FIRST IMPRESSIONS

When you join a new group, you have to make a great first impression. People will make a snap judgment of you in five seconds or less. How do you want to be remembered? Did you say something awkward to start a conversation? Did you smile? Did you forget someone's name? You only have a few seconds, so make it good! However, you must also be sincere and genuine. No one likes to be around fake people, and most people can judge you on your sincerity pretty quickly.

When you're at an event and ready to start a conversation, you say something along the lines of, "Hi, I'm Andrew." The other person responds by saying, "Hi, I'm Sarah." And then you respond by smiling and saying "pleasure to meet you." That's your five-second window of opportunity.

REMEMBERING NAMES AND STORIES

A key to making a great first impression is to remember people's names and aspects about their lives. I have a trick to help with this. I make a real effort to remember someone's name when I first hear it. I first introduce myself, then I let the person I'm talking with say his or her name, and then either I ask that person to repeat it, pretending I didn't hear it, or I repeat his or her name again, possibly using it in the first sentence of conversation. For example:

> *"Hi, I'm Andrew, pleasure to meet you. What's your name?"*
> *"John."*
> *"Ah, John, got it. Where are you from John?"*

In the first five seconds of conversation, I hear his name, had him say it and also included it in my first line of the conversation. The more you hear it and say it, the better your chances are of remembering his or her name.

And if you forget it, no big deal! Don't worry about it because they probably forgot your name too. At the end of the conversation, I would say something like, "It was so great meeting you. What was your name again?" If they forgot your name too, they'll probably feel relieved that you asked them that question.

Here's another trick—if you're out and about networking, ask for a business card after a few minutes of conversation. Taking a look at the card will also help you remember names because you're bringing in one more sense—your sight.

Need another trick? When you add people on Facebook or LinkedIn at an event, go back the next day and review who you just met and make a mental note of who they are, where they're from, where they went to school, what they studied, and anything else that's relevant. You don't have to remember their whole story, but if you can remember three to four critical details about each person, they will be impressed, as most people can't even remember your name. This trick in itself will make you stand out from the crowd; people will think you have such a good memory when in reality you just took some extra time to remember people's stories.

FRIENDS FIRST

I have a little policy I call "Friends First." When I go to a networking event, I approach new people I meet from the perspective that we must become friends first before anything else progresses with us, whether from a business perspective or on the social side. I have enough acquaintances in my life who stand there on the fringe and do their thing. I want real friends who have my back.

Perhaps you feel the same—you want people who will be there for you through good times and bad times. If your car breaks down, you want a friend who will come pick you up. If you just landed from a sixteen-hour flight from Australia, you want someone who will greet you at the airport. If you're sick, you want someone who will send you a get-well text. It's really not the big things that demonstrate real friendship, it's all the little things that prove who you are over time.

True friendships take time to evolve and mature. Just as in any relationship, you don't go from 0 to 100 mph overnight. And your time is the most valuable resource you have. As such, don't spend it on people, events, or activities that don't push you toward your goals in life.

WORDS OF CAUTION

Choose carefully. When you find yourself in the wrong crowd, your own sets of values go out the window. Therefore, you must be a) very careful of who you surround yourself with and b) highly selective of who you decide to engage in conversation with when you're out socializing.

Plan in advance. You can do a lot more in a given day when you have your days and weeks planned out. Whether you plan your week on Sunday nights or the night before, you must have a game plan! Things don't just magically happen—but you can make it look like it due to behind the scenes planning.

You don't have to get too crazy and plan out every minute of the day, but it definitely helps to either use a calendar and block periods of time off for certain activities or to at least have some type of schedule that will guide you. By using these systems, you can do more in less time, and ensure that you get out there.

TAKEAWAYS:

- Join a group or club—of any kind—that involves something you like to do or have never tried.

- The next time you meet someone new, practice saying their name back to them and using it within the next sentence.

- Keep a calendar—either in print or online—and start planning out your week!

Chapter 7

STEP FOUR: KNOW BEFORE YOU GO

When going to any event or place where there are people you're looking to meet, I highly suggest you do some research before you go. If you see a guest list and don't know who some people are, ask someone else or do a quick online search. Knowing a bit about who is at the event provides an easy conversation starter.

Life favors the prepared. When you're going somewhere and you know what you're getting yourself into, you're more likely than not to have a favorable outcome. The more prepared you are going into an event, the better you'll be at talking to people and striking up conversations.

If you're going to a huge convention with cardiologists, you sure better know your way around the heart; be able to talk about the latest trends, pressing issues, and any other news out there. The same can be said for any other type of event, convention, or activity. If you're going to play volleyball with some people you don't know, do your homework on volleyball and strike up conversations possibly about the Olympics, upcoming tournaments, leagues people play in, or anything else that is relevant. By doing the research, it shows that you are in fact interested in whatever activity or event you're attending (even if you're not). Furthermore, it helps you to feel comfortable and confident in your conversations versus being shy and timid because you don't know a damn thing about hearts!

On that note, I highly encourage you to attend events you know nothing about. It's the easiest way to meet people outside of your own network. Just make sure you have something to add to the conversation, or you'll be walking out shortly because people will think you're there for the wrong reasons. Figure out a way to tie in why you're there to make it relevant to the rest of the group. Just like any tribe, people are willing to give you a shot if they think you're like them. That's the easiest way to become part of the group – it's group thinking 101. If you look like me, dress like me, talk like me, and sound like me, I'll feel more comfortable accepting you as one of us even if your real job has nothing to do with the group.

SURVEY THE ROOM

Once you're there, take a step back and look around at the people in the room. You'll be able to see the life of the party person, the host, the person who has OCD and is all over the place putting out fires, the lush, the dancer, the creeper, and so on. Before fully engaging in conversations, take the time to do your homework and at least look over the room for a couple of minutes to see where you want to start.

It's much harder to walk away with new friends if you don't have a game plan of who you want to talk to. Do you go straight for the host? Do you want to dance first? Do you talk to people you know first? Have a plan and stick to it, and you'll have much better success making friends and meeting who you want to meet.

KNOW WHERE TO GO

The other part of "know before you go," is determining what a good event is and what is not. This too will take time. The more you become involved in your community, the more you'll get a feel for what to attend and what not to attend. If you're skeptical, ask someone for feedback. Or if that's not available, do some of your own research to see and hear what others have said.

A GUIDELINE TO HELP YOU MANAGE YOUR TIME AND EXPERIENCE AT EVENTS

1. Assess the situation:

   a. Who's there that you want to talk to?

   b. Who do you know?

   c. Who's open to having a conversation?

   d. Who do you want to avoid?

2. Go talk to the person or persons on your highest priority list, or if they're occupied, strike up a conversation with who on your target list is open to talking or one of your friends. Take action, rather than just standing there and expecting people to come talk to you. People like people who are assertive.

3. Be friendly, smile, and be yourself. Whoever you're talking with, strike up a genuine conversation and have your "go-to questions" ready to go. These are your five to ten questions

you can pull at your disposal for any given conversation. (More on this in the next chapter.) Try to focus on the open-ended questions; make them talk about themselves, and open up a bit. That's the best approach to establishing a good rapport right from the start.

4. Close the conversation. After speaking to someone for a few minutes, either ask for a business card, get a phone number or add him or her on whatever social media platform you prefer. When closing conversations, I always say, "It was a pleasure to meet you," and if I want to maintain contact I say, "I will follow up at XYZ time in the future about having coffee, drinks, lunch, etc." But here's the catch—you MUST follow up with people if you say you are going to. You just made a great first impression, don't ruin it by not following up with them!

HOW TO MAXIMIZE THE NUMBER OF PEOPLE YOU MEET

You don't have to attend every single event you get invited to—that is literally impossible to do, only because there's not enough time in the day. However, there is a trick to at least look like you're accomplishing the impossible. You don't have to get too crazy and cram in three events in one night—but, you can try to do two events if they line up timing wise and in terms of proximity. It just takes some coordination. Example: if you're in one part of town for an event that goes from 5 to 8 p.m. and there's another event that goes from 6 to 9 p.m. in the same part of town, who says you can't do both? Go to the first event from 5 to 7 p.m., then cut out and go to the second event from 7:30 to 9 p.m. You will be able to meet twice as many people this way because you went to two different events with hopefully a different crowd at each.

How do you meet as many people as possible at each event? Peg your conversations for two to three minutes; depending on who you're talking to, there may be some conversations you choose to extend to five minutes. After that, it's time to move on. I know it seems a bit odd or awkward to meet someone, get all their information, and then gracefully exit the conversation, but that's the beauty of networking and socializing. It's not a first date.

If you meet someone you know you want to spend more time with later, ask if they have a business card (rule number one when you're out networking—ALWAYS carry a business card!) Sometimes there are people you don't want to give your card to, which is fine. You can always say, "I'm so sorry, I just ran out, but I can take yours." Is that reasonable to do? Absolutely. If you don't want people who make you feel uncomfortable following up with you, then give them that line.

Once you have their card, wrap up the conversation by asking about doing lunch or coffee the following week. Boom! The conversation was ended in five minutes or less and you are free to go make more connections.

HOW TO EXIT A DULL CONVERSATION

One question I'm sure you've asked yourself is, "How do I exit conversations with people who keep on talking and talking, who I want nothing to do with?" Easy. There's usually three options I like to use:

1) If you're at an event where you have some mutual acquaintances, pull them into the conversation with the infamous, "Have you met my friend?" line. Your friend might not be too keen on this, but if you get them started in conversation, then you can excuse yourself from the

conversation from there. Who knows—maybe your friend will hit it off with the person you were talking to.

2) If I see someone I recognize, I interrupt the conversation and say, "I'm so sorry, my friend Tim just got here and I have to go say hi to him. It was so nice talking to you and I look forward to catching you at the next event," or something along those lines. Extend your hand for a handshake, and gracefully exit. Once you present your hand, it's awkward not to shake it, so it's usually the easiest way to get out of a conversation.

3) Find an excuse to get out, such as, "I have to go use the restroom, you'll have to excuse me." You could try, "I have to make a call," or "Excuse me, I forgot I had to send an email to my boss. It was a pleasure meeting you," and then exit from there.

4) If worst comes to worst, you just have to interrupt them, and say "John, it's been a pleasure talking to you. I have to work the room, so I have to excuse myself, but wish you the best." Is it rude? Not really. You shouldn't have to waste your time talking to people you don't want to talk to.

WORDS OF CAUTION

It's not about the numbers. Don't have too high of expectations. When you go somewhere and expect to meet fifty people and only walk away having met five, you'll be disappointed. Just like when you go to an event or an outing with a few friends or new friends, don't set the bar at an unreachable level.

I like to go to events with little or no expectations. That way, whatever experience I have will be better than anything I had thought. When you go out, base your experience on the quality of people you meet and not the sheer number. It's better to meet real friends who make an effort to keep in touch and who will be there for you.

Be highly selective of who's in your inner circle of friends. It's a funneling process. You start with 100 people and you funnel that down to 30 acquaintances, then to 10 friends, and then to 1 or 2 best friends. I like to put my friends into three tiers:

1. Inner circle group of friends—10 people or less

2. Regular friends who I see on a somewhat consistent basis—can be any number because all of our friendships are different, and for some a few years can go by before we see each other again

3. Acquaintances—people who I know, but don't know well or I haven't been able to get a read on them yet. They're nice people, but on the outer fringe because I don't allow people I barely know to encroach on my regular friends or inner circle group of friends.

TAKEAWAYS:

- Before you attend any event, do a quick Google search to learn more about the topic, the host organization, etc. This will help you have relevant go-to questions ready and make it easier for you to fit in and engage with others.

- Have a game plan for each event you attend. Who do you want to meet? Who do you want to talk to?

- Peg your conversations at events to two or three minutes—no longer than five minutes. This will give you time to meet more people!

Chapter 8

STEP FIVE: MASTER THE INTRODUCTION

ASK THE RIGHT QUESTIONS

If you're in a room of 100 people for a networking event, how will you separate yourself from everyone else? How will you standout from the crowd? Asking the same tired old question of "what do you do" will bore people and immediately they'll put you in a bucket with the other fifty people who just asked them the same question. No one wants to repeat themselves fifty times in a matter of two hours. So be original! Come up with something that fits your persona and your style.

You must build rapport with people to establish relationships. Start out with some warm, soft questions such as, "How did you hear about this event?" or "Who else do you know here?" or "What do you think of the venue?" or any other open-ended question. I do like to ask if it is their first time at the event or activity as well, as that's my way to gauge the conversation and steer it in whatever direction I want to steer it.

I like to think of starting a conversation as a research project. I can't really have an engaging conversation with someone unless I ask a lot of questions that don't have simple yes or no answers. At the same time, I can't have the conversation turn into an interrogation. Do you want to play a game of twenty questions? I know I don't.

Instead, ask the right questions about things people want to talk about, which is usually themselves! Ask them where they're from, where they live, how long they've lived in the city, if they've checked out any cool places recently, if they travel, or any topic that's relevant to current news and that does not involve politics or the weather. If you go into a conversation with an open mind, positive attitude, and an arsenal of questions you're ready to ask, then chances are you'll have a great conversation, and you will walk away with one new contact at the very least.

Here's a tip: If you want to ask about work, don't ask, "What do you do?" but instead ask, "What type of work are you in?" This simple shift in the question makes it not come off so cold and people don't feel as judged.

But no matter where you go, people will ask you, "What do you do?" If you're on the receiving end, you can have a funny answer. I have a friend who answers, "I'm a cat walker," or "I'm a sheep herder." You can tell the truth, or you can play with it.

HAVE YOUR QUESTIONS READY

What's your go-to conversation opener? Do you have a line? Do you say something cheesy, or do you just introduce yourself? First things first—stick to who you are. People easily pick up on your sincerity, so don't try to start a conversation by complimenting someone unless you genuinely mean it. Also, try not to repeat something this person has heard over and over. Be original if you're going to compliment, and start the conversation like you were talking to an old friend.

You should have a list of go-to questions memorized and ready to go at your disposal. Here are some examples:

STANDARD GO-TO QUESTIONS

1. How has your day been? Anything exciting happen?
2. Where are you from?
3. How long have you lived here?
4. How did you hear about this event?
5. Who do you know here? Who invited you?
6. When are they going to start serving food?
7. What's that you're drinking?
8. Have you been to these types of events before? If so, how was it?
9. I love that outfit, where did you get it from?
10. Which part of town do you live in?
11. Where do you usually go out on a Saturday night?
12. What time does the dance party start?
13. How's the food?
14. Where's the bar?
15. What type of work are you in?

As you can see from above, these are all very generic and easy questions to ask. Some are basic, some have depth, and others are just fillers or conversation exit questions, like "Where's the bar?" (Thanks, I'm going to head there now, it was great to meet you!)

Always keep in mind that people want to feel important. They want to talk about themselves. During the conversation, it is much better to listen and absorb information than to do all the talking. Once you get the conversation going, then start asking secondary questions that follow the first question you asked. This shows you are engaged in that conversation. If you follow this strategy, you'll become the best conversationalist in the room—regardless of whether you're truly committed to every conversation you're in or not.

CHEMISTRY

Now there's one thing you can't control: chemistry. You may have a lot in common with whoever you're talking to, but if there's no chemistry between the two of you then it's going to be pretty hard to maintain any conversation. Sometimes it's best to know when to cut your losses and move on.

How do you know if someone has chemistry with you? That's easy—if you're questioning whether you have chemistry or not, then you don't. It's an easy feeling to discern and something that should never be questioned.

I usually start a conversation for a few minutes to see where it goes. If after two or three minutes the conversation is stale and lacking any substance, I cut my losses and move on. If you want to pursue a conversation further that's up to you—to each his own. It takes time and practice to develop the skill of knowing when that point of walking away is. Just keep in mind that when you end a conversation, end it with grace by saying, "It was so nice to meet you." And of course, don't forget to smile!

HOW DO YOU STAND OUT?

How do you separate yourself from everyone else? What makes you special? When your best friend describes you, what stands out? Is it your witty sense of humor? How you dress? Your job? Your accent? These are all things I would take into consideration when you're going to an event. Sometimes you may just want to blend into the crowd, but perhaps there are times you want to stand out and use that to fuel conversation.

Here are a few friends of mine who stand out in different ways: Mark is an entrepreneur who really loves people. Instead of shaking hands with people, he hugs them. He prefaces this by telling that person that he's a hugger and then he goes straight in for the hug, leaving no time for the person to say no. Of course, some people may not like him invading their personal space, but it works for him and he sticks to it because that's who he is.

John, another friend of mine, prefers to shop in second-hand stores for clothes because he doesn't like other people to have the same clothes as him. He stands out by his appearance and his uniqueness when it comes to dressing.

Then there's my friend Audrey. She stands out because she wears her heart on her sleeve. She tells you how she feels and lays it all out in conversation and on social media. When you're with her you have no doubt about how she feels about you, because she'll tell you with love and compassion. Her words separate her apart from anyone else, as she's not afraid to be an open book.

Here are some tips to help you stand out:

1) Use open-ended questions and don't ask the same questions that everyone else already asked. Be original! Have your own line of questions ready to go so you're prepared to strike up a good conversation.

2) What you wear: You should always wear whatever you feel comfortable and confident in. However, you can stand out with your attire in many ways: It can be bold, it can be flashy, it can be something that's written on your shirt, or it can be really classy.

I normally pick my clothes based on how I'm feeling that day. Some days it's blue, some days it's purple or some days it's a pattern. I go with what I feel, because I know I'll be more confident in that color or outfit. Your clothes play a bigger role in your attitude than you may think. If you're comfortable, confident, and truly believe you look amazing in whatever you're wearing, that attitude becomes infectious.

HOW MEMORABLE DO YOU WANT TO BE?

There's a fine line between being the center of attention and having just enough fun. If you're at an event, say your friend's wedding, then no, you do not want to be the center of attention because it's not your day. That's just good etiquette. However, if you're at a networking event, it most likely doesn't hurt to be the center of attention; it's going to help you meet more people, and that's probably the main goal for the night.

Some people are extroverts, some introverts, and some are in the middle. Just because you're not an extrovert doesn't mean you can't be the center of attention. Sure, maybe you don't want attention, but how awesome would it be if people came to you to start conversations? You know what makes you special so use it!

If you're a good dancer, then find the opportunity to show off your dance moves. People will remember that. Or if you can play the piano, find somewhere to play. Just be you—people see through the fakeness all the time, so it's up to you to maintain your character, be genuine, and stick to who you are.

WORDS OF CAUTION

Though I do encourage you to dress in your own style and in what makes you feel comfortable and confident, be careful that you **dress to match whatever occasion you're at**. You don't want to show up to a polo match wearing a tank top and shorts.

If you're invited to a charity gala, then dress up! And guys, make sure your suit is tailored properly. The difference in fit is night and day—you don't want to look like a kid in an oversized suit. That piece is so critical and often gets overlooked. Spend some extra money and get your suit tailored – you'll thank me later!

TAKEAWAYS:

- Make a list of open-ended social questions you can have at your disposal, for the next time you meet someone new.

- If you don't feel chemistry with someone you just met, there is no need to continue the conversation. Exit politely with one of your readily-available escape lines.

- Think about what makes you unique. Is it your dance moves? Your style? Find an (appropriate) opportunity to emphasize it at the next event you attend.

Chapter 9

STEP SIX: MANAGE THE NON-VERBALS

ATTITUDE IS EVERYTHING

Why do you think certain people are able to accomplish things that seem impossible? Probably because they put on their poker face and pretend they've been there before. Some people have the confidence to walk into a private event that they weren't even invited to and start making friends immediately. How the hell did they do that?! Well, it's no secret really. It takes some courage, a bit of risk, and a bit of not caring what the consequences are. But beyond that, they pretended they knew what they were doing.

The same premise can apply to a variety of other topics, not just crashing weddings. There are many other people like you who are looking to make new friends. They're out at the same places, same events, same parties doing exactly what you're doing—trying to meet people! So instead of sitting on the fence at these events, pretend like you're a regular (even if you're not). Confidence is a big magnet for attracting people.

Having fun is also attractive. You're more open to meeting people when you're relaxed, smiling, and having a good time. If you have a blank stare on your face, are tight-lipped and not making eye contact when talking, you'll need to make some attitude adjustments if you want people to approach you.

Your entrance says a lot about who you are. What's your attitude when you enter a room? Do you walk in with your head held high and a smile on your face? Or do you walk in with slumped shoulders, no smile, and a nervous look on your face? Your look is the first thing people see, and your attitude is what creates your look.

Your tone, your voice, your appearance, and your body language all set the stage for you to gain interest and respect from others.

NON-VERBAL COMMUNICATION

How do you read other people's body language? Everyone is different, which means there is no one set of rules for how to read people. I find poker very interesting to watch; some people can read people better than others, and some have a much stronger poker face than others. Reading people is a science in its own right. There's body language, eye contact, handshakes, physical touch, laughter, and many more subtleties we can pay attention to. With practice, you will get better at assessing relationships and reading other people.

Some examples of body language signs you can easily read are as follows:

- Distance: How far is the person standing from you? Are they within arm's reach? Do they pull back when you touch them on the shoulder? Distance will tell you how engaged they are in the conversation and if they pull back when you touch them, there's a fair chance that they don't like you or they don't like you invading their personal space. As such, keep your distance but still be friendly, just without the touching.

- Sweat: Is the person sweating? As long as you're not somewhere hot, it most likely means they're nervous or have some anxiety. Make them feel at ease and warm them up with some friendly conversation by asking them questions about themselves.

- Eye Contact: Are they looking you in the eyes when you talk to them? Or are they gazing off somewhere else and not paying attention? They may be nervous, or they just might not be interested in talking to you. Give them one to two minutes to warm up, then ask them some questions and gauge their interest from there. If they're not interested in engaging in conversation, it's ok to say, "It was a pleasure," and walk off.

- Laughter/Smiling: If the person you're talking to is laughing or smiling as you are talking then you're doing great, of course! Either one is a good indicator that you're on the right track. On the opposite side, if the person you're talking to has little to no facial expression, that's not necessarily a bad thing, it just means you may have to work a little harder to get him or her engaged. If after a few minutes the person's facial expression hasn't changed from neutral, it's probably time to move on to someone else.

With any conversation you enter, you always start with a handshake and some form of "nice to meet you." At this point,

I think to myself, how did they shake my hand? Was it firm? Weak? Hand on top of mine? Limp-wristed? That tells me a lot about the person and whether they're confident or not.

Lastly, I gauge body positioning. Are they standing too close, too far, are they standing directly in front of me, or off to the side? There are certain instances where some of these are ok, but you definitely don't want to be right on top of someone you just met, as that puts them in an uncomfortable position.

As for your role, there are certain cues that invite people to come talk to you, versus you having to start your own conversations. First, start with a smile. No one wants to talk to someone with a frown or a scowl on his or her face. (Take a note that even when talking on the phone you should smile—people can actually hear you smile without even seeing you.)

Second, keep a good body position. This means you're not slouched, and you're standing upright. If talking with a group of people, don't close the circle off, leave space for others to join the conversation. If you're having an intimate conversation, then block yourselves off to try to keep others from joining. If you're having a one-on-one conversation, stand right in front of the person you're talking to; this will show that you're really engaged.

And make sure you have a solid handshake. It doesn't have to be overly firm, but just firm enough; it should line up with the other person's hand and not go below or on top of it. I'm not a prince and you're not a princess, so don't shake hands on top! And whether you're talking to a guy or a girl, the handshake needs to be solid because you're communicating your confidence through your hands, and through your touch. A weak handshake will diminish whatever you say right off the bat.

WHAT ABOUT PERSONAL TOUCH?

Whether or not to engage in personal touch is a delicate question. I like to touch people on the arms, the shoulders, and back when talking to them, but only in the right situations. How can you tell when it's the "right" situation? You have to gauge who you're talking to, if they're a man or a woman, and how well you know them. It takes time to develop an understanding of what's appropriate for one person versus another. Generally speaking, if you're going back and forth and having a great conversation, or if it's with someone you already know, then typically physical touch is not an issue.

For people you just met, hold off on the personal touches, as some people take offense or feel awkward and uncomfortable. The more you're able to read people, the better you'll see who you can and who you can't touch when having a conversation. I think it does add in a special element of care and trust when you're talking to your friends and put your arm around them— or even give them a fist bump. That still counts for something!

I like to think that positive energy can be conveyed through touch, which is why when I shake someone's hand, I usually put my left hand on his or her shoulder or upper back and say "good to see you." That's not for everyone, but in certain situations it can be welcomed and appreciated. In the world we live in today, people have become more distant due to technology. Leveraging personal touch can put you at an advantage, because not everyone is good at communicating with it. When you master personal touch, people will feel more connected to you and your conversations will feel more engaging. Just start off easy, lean on the side of caution, and go with it from there.

Also worth nothing are cultural differences. Do your research before traveling to foreign countries. In some countries, it's courtesy to kiss on the check once when you greet each other. In some countries it's twice. Some cultures are very cold and only use a hand shake, with no physical touch beyond that. Knowledge is power and you don't want to start on the wrong foot by violating cultural norms when it comes to traveling abroad.

TAKEAWAYS:

- Feeling uncomfortable walking into an event? Pretend you've been there before. Confidence goes a long way in attracting people to you and easing the discomfort.

- Smile, stand upright, and have a solid handshake.

- When first meeting someone, shy away from personal touch. As you develop your ability to read people, you will know when or if it's appropriate to communicate with a small gesture of touch.

Chapter 10

STEP SEVEN: FOLLOW UP / FOLLOW THROUGH

This step is in regards to being an effective communicator—which requires following up to messages in a timely manner and expressing your thoughts and feelings concisely and consciously. Sounds easy enough, right? Well, unfortunately, that's not so much the case these days. In today's digital world, we are inundated with messages from all over—via email, text messages, Facebook, phone calls, Tweets, Snapchat, LinkedIn, and whatever else you can think of. How do you find the time to respond to all these messages? And what's important enough to respond to?

My first piece of advice here is to learn how to prioritize. What comes first should be different during the week and also at different times of the day. When you're working from 8 a.m. to 6 p.m. you should be focusing on work, that's a given. As you're constantly getting pinged from multiple sources, it may be best to put away your cell phone so you're not distracted, and to wait to respond to those messages at lunchtime or anytime you take a bathroom break.

One way to prioritize communication with friends, family, and co-workers is based on the way people contact you. Here's my list from most urgent to least urgent:

1. Phone call – if friends or family are calling you, it would seem pretty important or urgent.

2. Text message – if you need to reach a friend, this is probably the best route to go. I don't have much time to chat on the phone, and suspect you don't either.

3. Email – if something is urgent, people don't typically resort to email.

4. Social media messages – if someone sends you a message through Facebook, it probably means he or she doesn't have your phone number, so how good of friends are you?

5. Paper mail / other – this may not be the most glamorous form of communication and yes, it may be outdated, however people still like to receive mail. If you want to stand out, I highly recommend writing a few notes per week to a handful of people. It will be worth the postage, as your friends will be surprised to receive anything that's not junk, and you'll make their day. In terms of urgency, however, paper mail ranks last.

MANAGING YOUR COMMUNICATION TIME

How do you find the time to respond to so many messages? There truly is only so much time in a day, and you do need to eat, sleep, go to work, spend time with your partner and so on. However, you have to train your brain to understand that spending ten seconds to respond to a text message is not time-consuming.

True, there are distractions coming at us 24/7, but it's all a matter of how we manage them. We all have jobs to do and responsibilities to take care of, and sometimes you have to put your phone away to focus on the task at hand. What helps me is to make a note, whether in a draft email or somewhere on my computer, in regards to who I need to follow up with later in the day.

Learn how to maximize your time. When walking to the bathroom, respond to a text message. When using public transportation, write an email. When going for a walk, make a phone call. Use these tricks to maximize your time so you can respond to people as quickly and efficiently as possible. Instead of trolling through social media on your walk in from the parking lot to work, shoot a text message to a friend. They'll appreciate the effort—especially if it's not the typical, "Hey, what's up?" or "Have a great day!" text message. Put some substance in your communication—something with extra thought, that is deeper than the surface level clutter we hear every day.

KNOW HOW MUCH IS TOO MUCH OR TOO LITTLE

Good friends stay in regular contact, whether that's once a day or once a week or once a month, it doesn't really matter. What matters is that you make an effort to stay in touch consistently. I have friends who live in Europe, and we might email each other a handful of times in a given year. Does that make us bad friends? Nope! It means we're comfortable with our friendship and we're ok with the level of communication between us.

Of course, you may suggest otherwise but that's okay—we are all individuals with different ways of doing things. You know what's best for you and your friends, and I know what's best for me and my friends; every relationship and friendship has its own set of quirks. It's up to you to read and understand your relationships to know how much contact is too much, and how much is too little.

CUSTOMIZE YOUR COMMUNICATION

Everyone is different, so it's tough to know what kind of communication is best amongst friends and acquaintances. The trick is to cater not only your communication method to every person you talk to, but the tone, dialogue, and length of conversation. Some people prefer to text. Some prefer to call. Some prefer short conversations. Some prefer to talk your ear off. To make an impression, you have to know your audience.

To be an effective communicator, all you really have to do is make an effort and be consistent regarding how often you talk to people. Reading people, body language, and physical touch, collectively all play a part in effective communication too. Generally speaking though, it really comes down to making an effort. Don't wait for someone else to call or text you. Call a friend. Send a text. You never know what the response will be until you ask. Don't psyche yourself out. Who cares if they say no? Or if they're already busy. Try someone else. Make the effort, and then watch what happens.

If someone doesn't reply or follow through with a plan, life just got easier for you, because you've automatically weeded out those who don't make the cut as one of your best friends.

GUIDELINE TO WRITTEN FOLLOW-UP

It's one thing to tell someone you'll be in touch, but it's another to actually do it. You will stand far and above most other people by actually following through with that statement. Make that extra effort and people will appreciate you as a friend, a contact, and someone who is willing to go the extra mile.

Most initial follow-up is done through a written format, such as email. If you customize your email a little bit too and reference something about a conversation you've had together, that will help you stand out.

We all lead busy lives, from sunup, to sundown, and into the night. There's constant pressure to "be on." As such, it is critical that you learn to communicate your message in the most effective way, and secondarily with the least amount of words. Most people don't have time to read a two-paragraph text or the equivalent of a three-page email.

If you have something that is super long to text or email, pick up the phone and call the person. And yes, sometimes emails have to be long—just don't make it a habit. Get to the point, say what you have to say, and move on. Here's a general guideline for length of communication:

1. Text messages – keep them short, preferably 140 characters or less. Definitely don't text more than a screen's worth of information, as no one wants to scroll to read your message.

2. Emails – same premise. Keep them to one screen if possible, and ideally a few paragraphs at most.

3. Phone calls – it depends on what the topic is, but you can probably get your point across in five minutes or less. At least for me, unless it's my girlfriend, family

member, or a conference call for work, I really don't want to spend an hour with someone on the phone.

4. Social media messages – these follow text messaging rules. Keep them short and preferably 140 characters or less.

WORDS OF CAUTION

Don't Be a Flake. That is the premise of following up and following through. Friends are naturally there for each other, and if you don't respond to their messages or if you don't show up when you're supposed to, then what kind of friend are you? Expect the same level of care and attention from yourself that you would expect from others.

Be honest with your friends. If you don't want to go somewhere, say it. There's no need to tell your friends you can be somewhere if you know you can't. They'll appreciate your honesty and if they don't, then they're probably not very good friends themselves. The foundation of friendship is based on trust and honesty. Demonstrate these qualities yourself, and expect the same in return.

TAKEAWAYS:

- Prioritize the steady stream of messages you receive based on the method they were sent.

- When you meet people you connect with, shoot them a follow-up message the next day.

- Stay true to your word—it's your bond. If you make plans, stick to them. Don't back out at the last minute.

Chapter 11

STEP EIGHT: ACTIONS SPEAK LOUDER THAN WORDS

*"On my honor I will do my best
To do my duty to God and my country
and to obey the Scout Law;
To help other people at all times;
To keep myself physically strong,
mentally awake, and morally straight."*

The above oath comes from the Boy Scouts, and it helped shape me into the man I am today. I grew up a Cub Scout and made my way into the Boy Scouts before growing older and focusing more on high school sports and socializing. However, by the time I was in high school I had repeated the oath above too many times to count and because of that, it totally changed me as a person without me even knowing it.

I always help other people and put others first before my own needs. When you put others first and help them however you can, that sounds like a pretty easy and fast way to make friends, right? Exactly! According to Scout Law, "A Scout is trustworthy, loyal, helpful, friendly, courteous, kind, obedient, cheerful, thrifty, brave, clean, and reverent." In fact, those are all traits I would use to describe my best friend. If you're able to prove time and time again that you are more than willing and able to help someone else out, then you've proven yourself as a good friend.

Have you ever taken an oath? If so, what was it for? A job? The military? A club? Imagine if there were an oath that friends had to take in order to be friends. Wouldn't that make life much simpler? In this day and age, it is very hard to discern people's intentions. Who's good? Who's bad? Who's looking out for their own interests only? I wish there were an easy way to tell. Unfortunately, this one is on you. It's up to you to gauge your friends, to learn who they really are and to determine if they're really a true friend or just an acquaintance.

My biggest advice here is to not jump to conclusions about who is a good friend, just like I wouldn't recommend you jump to any conclusion about your boyfriend or girlfriend. I've known people who had just met their significant other, and in a matter of two months they were moving in together and talking about getting married. Call me old-fashioned, but that's not for me. Do you think you can find out everything about a person in one, two, or three months? It doesn't matter if you're spending every waking second with that person; it takes time to reveal everything there is to know about someone.

The same goes for friends. You can meet a person, think he or she is awesome, become new best friends, and boom, six months later that new best friend vanishes into thin air for whatever reason and you're back to square one. Friendships are like roller coasters – there are ups, downs, twists, turns, and inverted dives. You want to find those friends that are always ready to ride with you no matter what. Good friends stick together through thick and thin and have each other's back. Loyalty goes a long way these days, as I think it's something that has been forgotten over time.

ARE YOUR ACTIONS IN ALIGNMENT?

With the amount of technology in our hands today, words seem to have gained more value than actions. However, I would have to argue that words still hold little value compared with actions. If you want to be a good friend, then your actions will solidify who you are and words will remain just what they are – words. Words are really just thin air that people can use to describe themselves, but people are judged more by what they do than what they say.

Now that doesn't give you the right to go around saying things that are meaningless. Rather, you have to combine the two together – whatever you say has to match whatever you do. If you tell a friend you're going to be there in a time of need and your friend calls and says they need you, you'd better be there for him or her. The things you say and do over time will determine how people view who you are. Are you trustworthy? Do you care? Will you be there when you say you'll be there? Are you punctual? Do you promise one thing and do another? You are bound by your words.

For example, if you make a promise to volunteer at a charity event but don't follow through and put the time and effort in, people won't want to hang out with you. They'll think of you as a flake, undependable, and unreliable. You must build your reputation and your credibility first and foremost. Your reputation precedes you – therefore you have to put in the time and effort to build it up.

Help out a friend in need. Go out of your way to make you friend's day. Remember birthdays, favorite foods, holidays, or anything really...these are all ways to prove that you're a great friend with a good heart and great character.

BE A GIVER AND A RECEIVER

All good, solid relationships are built on a two-way street. There's a give and take to friendships, a push and pull feeling. If I do something for you, then at some point you'll do something for me in return. You never want to find yourself in a one-sided relationship, because eventually you'll get sick and tired of carrying the load and that relationship or friendship will fade into the sunset. However, being a giver should never feel like work. You should do things naturally for each other because you want to, not because you have to.

When was the last time you did something thoughtful for one of your friends? You can start by doing something nice today! Being nice doesn't cost anything; it can be the smallest gesture. Doing something special for your friends will leave a lasting impact and feeling with them, and that's something you can't put a price tag on. How you make people feel is priceless.

TAKEAWAYS:

- If you say you're going to be there for someone or something, be there. Your actions should match your words.

- If you have a friend who consistently initiates plans, give them a break—reach out to them with a plan of your own!

- Do something nice for a friend today—it doesn't have to cost anything.

Chapter 12

STEP NINE: BE REAL, BE GENUINE, BE YOURSELF

What's the easiest way to meet people? Be you. Plain and simple. Long-lasting relationships and friendships are built on being genuine. If you want someone to be your friend for years and years, they're going to have to like you for who you are down to your core. What does genuine mean, exactly? It means that you care, you're honest, sincere, you have nothing to hide and you're not trying to be something you're not. Well, at least that's my definition.

When you're trying to be someone you're not, it's a bit difficult to hold an intellectual conversation. Maybe you can pull it off, but after awhile it gets old because the longer you go, the harder it gets to maintain the fake persona. And why would you want to bother being someone else in the first place? You're awesome, and don't let anyone else ever tell you otherwise! When you're in your own shoes, it's much easier to have a conversation, to be at your best, to be relaxed, and to be able to talk about whatever subject comes up. When you're trying to fake who you are, being social just becomes more of a job, and when it's a job it's not any fun at all.

My rule of thumb in being yourself is that it starts out with how you dress. Wear comfortable clothes that make you feel confident. If you're wearing an outfit that you don't like, your game will be off from the get-go. Your conversations will lack substance because you'll be more focused on your outfit than the people you're meeting.

People are happiest when they are being themselves, not when they're trying to imitate someone else—whether that's how they talk, how they look, where they shop, what they eat, or any other variety of things.

BE HONEST

Honesty really is the only way. Telling the truth isn't just about being honest, it's the feeling that goes with it; it's about having a clear conscience. It's about going to bed at night not worrying about if people are going to find out if you lied.

It's much easier to just tell the truth, accept the consequences for anything you did and move on with life. This all goes back to the very first chapter in the book where I talked about the two most important questions: Do you care? Can I trust you?

Obviously, you can't be trusted if you don't tell the truth. It can take years to build up your reputation and only seconds to for it to crumble under one lie. That's why it's critical for you to maintain your character at all times, to be ethical, and to be honest. I know there are many temptations out there, but it's up to you to live up to your own personal code of conduct and to adhere to being honest every single day.

BE CREATIVE

What do you do when you get that dreaded question, "How do I look?" Whether the question is from one of your friends or a spouse, you still need to be honest, but you can be creative. You don't have to be brutally honest about it, as there's a dance you can do in these instances.

For example, when asked that question in regards to an outfit I don't care for, I'll say "I think you look better in that other outfit," or "I really like you in the first one you tried on." It's the power of positive thinking and not being so critical. No one wants to hear that he or she looks bad, or fat, or ugly. And it's not your place to say it, even if you think it. Instead just dance around the subject, make a positive statement and tell that person he or she looks better in another outfit. And if you keep getting pressed on why, just say you like the first style better, or it just fits better, or you prefer the color, or the look, or whatever. There are plenty of ways to avoid offending people in situations like this without having to lie. You just have to be a bit creative.

BE AUTHENTIC

Making sacrifices for friends is a nice gesture as well, as long as it doesn't get out of hand. Again, the principle of a two-way street is most relevant here. Good friends do not take advantage of each other and you should never feel that you're giving everything you can to a friendship and getting little to nothing in return.

If you ever have any issues with your friends, just be up front about it. If you've been holding onto something for a very long time, the other person most likely has no clue that there is an issue. When you bring it up five years down the road, it becomes a very difficult and awkward conversation.

There is nothing wrong with having candid conversations about what's on your mind, and your friends should appreciate that and respect it. Effective communication is a must between good friends; if you're not communicating then your friendship is bound to only last for so long. And by communicating, I'm referring to in person talks versus texting, emailing, or phone calls. Real conversations happen in person. It is much easier to read a person when you're face to face versus any other type of outlet.

YOU DO YOU

It's imperative that you ask yourself routinely, what's really important to you? Is it your family, friends, your job, money, hobbies, or something else? Until you determine what you value you the most, it's hard to gauge how much time you should be dedicating to certain activities.

Have a heart to heart with yourself. Take some time to remove yourself from the outside world—no distractions, no phone, no internet. Go out in nature and take a walk, ride a bike, do something outdoors. Think about what's important in your life and what you value.

I remember a conversation I had with David, my best friend and former roommate back in college. We asked each other, what do you value? We had very different responses, to say the least. He valued his relationship with his girlfriend (now his wife), along with doing well in school, traveling, and his family. I valued food, socializing, traveling, and generally having a good time. There are no right or wrong answers, but it helped to speak with my best friend about values and what's important in life. I highly encourage you to do the same, either with your best friend or on your own. It will help you get some clarity; if making friends isn't one of your values, at least you'll be true to yourself and focus on whatever is important to you.

This whole exercise is one of the best ways to get to know yourself. Too often we try to conform to other people's standards of who we should be versus who we truly are. Our parents want us to grow up to be doctors, lawyers, or bankers. Great – but is that who we really are? Probably not. One of my favorite mantras is, "You do you." March to your own beat and never look back or even to the side. Trust yourself, that whatever path you choose is the best path for you. If you think about it, who knows you better than yourself? No one!

BE SELFISH

I always like to ask who comes first? Answer: me! Sounds very selfish, right? Well, there are times in life where you need to be selfish. Time is something you can never get back; manage your time wisely and spend it with people who matter to you, doing things you want to do.

My general philosophy in life and in meeting friends is to be a "yes" man or a "yes" woman – but how do we say no to things we don't want to do? There is a fine line between just saying yes and doing random things that don't matter to you, versus saying no to things you're not genuinely interested in. Trust your gut and if someone asks you to do something that you're not comfortable with or just don't want to do, then say no. If they get mad that's their problem, not yours. Why? Because you come first!

KNOW YOUR INTENTIONS

The tone of voice, the topic of conversation, the body language, and overall level of confidence you bring to the table will determine if you pass the smell test when you first meet a potential new friend. You want people to think you're a good person with good intentions—so what *are* your intentions?

People can see through you easily. If your intentions are to sell, then guess what? That's what people are going to see first. If you're there to meet someone from the opposite sex, that's what people will notice first. Don't think you're fooling anyone. You may think you're the smoothest, slyest person out there, but you're not. I'm a big believer in that what you put out is what you get in return. If you're willing to go out of your way to help someone, then that's what will come back to you.

You don't always have to have intentions either. It's perfectly fine to show up somewhere just to hang out, or to meet people in general. I think that's probably what the majority of people do. Just be aware of your surroundings and know what you're getting yourself into.

WORDS OF CAUTION

Know your worth. Never be desperate for friends. People can sense it, feel it, and see it. It's hard to make friends if you come off desperate and start smothering people with a million questions and asking them what they're doing six months down the road. Ease up! Just like if you're pursuing a guy or girl, don't rush into things, and don't scare people off in the first few minutes of a conversation.

Take a deep breath, relax, be yourself, and have a natural conversation. Pretend like you have 500 friends even if you don't. Fake it until you make it.

Never settle. There's no reason why you should ever settle on your friends. People should like you because of who you are, not what you do or what you own. If people only hang out with you because of your status, then those aren't real friends at all and you should re-evaluate who you surround yourself with.

I'd rather be by myself than be with fake friends. There is absolutely nothing wrong with being on your own for a certain period of time. Sometimes we need that time to find ourselves, our desires, what we really aspire to be in life—and to determine what we are looking for in our friends.

TAKEAWAYS:

- Stay true to who you are. You can only pull off a fake persona for so long before it backfires.

- Have a heart to heart with yourself. What is *really* important to you? What do you value? Live your life accordingly.

- Remember, no matter what: You come first.

Chapter 13

STEP TEN: STEP OUTSIDE YOUR COMFORT ZONE

Two of the best ways I've found to step outside my comfort zone include dancing and traveling overseas by myself. Interestingly, these are two of the best ways I've found to make new friends as well. When we step outside our comfort zone, new pathways are created in our brain, and therefore in our behavior. If you've been having a hard time making friends, you need to engage in a new behavior.

DANCE LIKE NO ONE IS WATCHING

Have you ever attended a wedding or been at a club or party and seen that one person out there dancing to the music by themselves? Think about it—who do people generally remember, the first person to do something, or the last? It's the first person because people generally perceive the first person to do something as someone who is brave—someone who is not afraid of being watched and being judged. If you're out there dancing, smiling and having fun, people will gravitate towards you because they naturally want to be around others who are having fun.

If you choose to experiment with dancing as a way to step outside your comfort zone and make friends note that there are a few caveats to consider. The first is that you have to be at least an okay dancer. If you're the first one out on the dance floor and you're not in sync with the music, others may not want to join you. You can still go out dancing if you have no rhythm— but don't be the first guy or girl out on the dance floor. It's much easier to dance in your own style when there are other people already dancing so no one will probably notice.

If you fall into the latter category, however, a better option is to take some dance lessons. It doesn't matter if it's hip-hop, country, ballroom, swing, or any other style. Taking dance lessons will give you the confidence needed to own the dance floor. In addition, dance classes are a great way to meet people— everyone is learning together in a supportive environment that is conducive to one-on-one interaction. Partner dance classes remove some of the initial social awkwardness of meeting new people, because you automatically exchange names at the start of each dance, you have a given transition into further questioning (how long have you been dancing/have you taken other dance classes before?), and a shared interest in learning to become better dancers.

A second caveat to being the first one out on the dance floor is: Don't be arrogant about your dance moves. If you can dance and dance well, awesome! But don't do it to gain accolades or attention – dance like a star because that's just how you dance. It's who you are. If you show off too much, then you will only isolate yourself because everyone else will be too intimidated to join you—or will be too repulsed by your arrogance.

The third and final caveat: If you're a guy, don't bump and grind with the girls. This isn't 1999 and you're not R. Kelly. Dance side-to-side with girls. It's less intimidating, girls respect that, and it will come off much more in a playful, fun, and genuine manner. Have you ever seen the look on a girl's face when a stranger starts dancing behind her? Don't be that guy. The idea is to make friends, right? No one wants to be friends with that guy. When you dance side-to-side, girls can see you coming; if they don't want to dance with you, they can easily walk away because you've danced in a non-threatening manner.

Learning how to dance can give you the confidence to do a number of things outside of the dance world. Imagine that you're doing a dance performance in front of 100+ other dancers and you have the whole stage to showcase your moves. Are you nervous? Or do you enjoy the thrill of performing and having that adrenaline rush? If you can make it through this, you can do anything you set your mind to, whether that's public speaking, talking to the opposite sex, asking for a promotion, or anything that takes courage. Dancing gives you more than you can imagine, and I highly encourage you to take it up and work on those skills.

If dancing really isn't your thing, the whole concept of social dancing can be applied to any other activity. Take kickball for example—if you're looking to meet other people around your age in a fun, social environment, then join a kickball team. You don't have to be the best kickball player out there, but to be social you have to get out and do something, whether it's dancing, kickball, joining a running club or a book club. Just get out there and start seeing what works for you!

LIVE A LIFE WELL TRAVELED

To stay in one place your entire life is to live in a vacuum. Just like a ship that stays in a harbor, you're always safe. But that's not how life is meant to be. A ship wasn't built to stay at the dock and you weren't put on this earth to stay in the same town or city all of your life.

Get out of your comfort zone, explore, be adventurous—even if you only travel an hour away. That still counts for something. The more you travel, the more people you meet along your journeys, and in turn, the more friends you'll make. There are an infinite number of places in the world to see and experience.

Take a solo trip or two abroad, if you haven't already. It will change your life forever; you'll make new friends from around the world, and you'll get to see places that most people never get to see. One of the biggest bonuses you'll get from traveling solo is a major confidence boost. One reason to travel abroad is for the adventure, another reason is to learn about who you are and what you can handle. You will face situations while traveling where you have to think on your toes, adapt very quickly, and learn how to survive. These are all good life lessons that cannot be taught in the classroom.

Apart from life lessons learned, how great would it be to have friends on nearly every continent around the world? It's not that hard to achieve once you start traveling and socializing abroad. And don't worry if you don't have thousands of dollars; once you pay for the airfare, these trips don't have to be that expensive. I highly recommend staying in hostels when you travel abroad. With technology, you can read reviews to find good hostels anywhere in the world that will probably run around $20-30 a night for a shared room with four to six other backpackers.

By staying in hostels versus Airbnb rentals or hotels, you will meet so many random people from around the world. Sure, there are times where you'll get stuck in a room with someone who snores, someone who smells, or someone who may be a questionable character, but you will learn to roll with the punches. Just keep an eye on your valuable items and you'll be fine—99% of hostels have lockers to put your valuables in anyway.

By traveling alone, you will meet people who are also looking to make friends. You don't need to plan much of an itinerary, nor do you have to wing it. Come with a basic plan, but be flexible because you're going to meet others in the hostel who will invite you to various activities. Before you know it, you'll join forces, take some tours, have dinner together and become friends. When you're by yourself, you will have the flexibility that is not offered when you're traveling in a group or in pairs. It also forces you to get out of your comfort zone; you have to talk to new people—whether you speak their language, or not. Otherwise, it will be a very lonely trip.

In fact, I encourage you to seek out people who are *not* native English speakers. If you're American, make it a point not to hang out with too many Americans—you can do that back in the U.S.! Make friends with the locals, ask them where to go, or if you can tag along on any of their outings. The trip should be about having new experiences, and the people, the culture, the food, the language. Immerse yourself in whatever city you're staying in so that when you depart, you'll leave with pictures, stories, new friends, and probably plans for your next trip.

THE BEST OF BOTH WORLDS

To mix the best of both worlds, take dance classes while traveling abroad! I took a salsa dance class while traveling in New Zealand, met a girl from Austria who was in the class and ended up getting invited to go out dancing with her in Austria. I can't say no to foreign girls, so we made plans and a year later we danced around Salzburg for a few days together.

Technology makes it really easy to stay in touch-and to communicate across language barriers. Thanks to Google Translate, you can put your smartphone on international roaming and poof! You can have a conversation via the app. Type in what you're saying in English, and have it translated over to Portuguese, or speak into the app and have it translated via voice.

Aside from the ability to converse in person, it's easy to communicate with people across the world via WhatsApp or to message people on Facebook. Fifteen years ago Facebook didn't even exist, nor did smartphones, so there wasn't an easy way to keep in touch with people outside of email. Now? It's really too easy. You can make friends with people from all over the world, keep in touch, and travel the world on a budget—many times you'll be invited to stay for free in your new friend's home. Before you know it, you'll have 100 friends spread out around the globe from Australia to Dubai, to Moscow, to Buenos Aires. The world is your playground, use it often and make friends wherever you go.

Tracee has been my best friend for five years now, but we first met through salsa dancing and have taken numerous trips together now. She also helps out in a number of areas for New Town Connections. Here is her story:

CASE STUDY: TRACEE

Being a part of New Town Connections has done more for me than I could ever have imagined. As a girl who was born and raised in the Tampa Bay area since birth, one would think that I would have had hundreds of childhood friends to continue making lasting memories with as an adult. In fact, my experience was the exact opposite.

The few friends I made from my Catholic High School moved away for college, never to return, and the few that stayed went their own way over time. As a result of my limited friendship circle, I opted to focus my attention on work and my education. However, over time I found myself not only overworked but somewhat lonely.

I soon discovered an interest in salsa dancing, which became my outlet to the social world and over the next two and a half years it became my WORLD outside of work. I later found that although salsa dancing was exciting and fun, it also had its limits. I loved to dance, go to salsa congresses, and also go on salsa cruises, but in the end, I had forged no real bonds with the individuals within that scene. Although amazing people, I did not know how to go about making connections with those people beyond dancing.

I did, however, meet Andrew Machota through the salsa community, who changed the game of life for me forever. Over time, Andrew not only became my amazing dance partner but also my dearest friend. Then Andrew had a vision and later made me a part of that vision, and I never looked back. The vision was New Town Connections and the goal was simple, but the reward was priceless.

The vision of New Town Connection was to create an environment for young professionals to meet through creative activities, and to forge lasting friendships. As adults, we meet people in our professional world all the time and if we are lucky enough, we may develop a few friendships as a result of those interactions. Outside of the work world, however, where does an adult go to meet people? A club? Local bar? Work function? For me, very few "friends" came out of those interactions with co-workers.

With my involvement in New Town Connections, I have cultivated true friendships with people I can call on in a time of need. Though I have lived in Tampa my entire life, I'd never really seen

Tampa for what it is... a growing city full of life and culture. I would have never discovered my home city if it were not for New Town Connections offering me the opportunity to do so, and to be able to do it with the amazing friends that I now have.

WORDS OF CAUTION

Activities like dancing can be a great way to meet people, but if you get sucked in, it's hard to get out. That's not necessarily a bad thing—you may find a great sense of community or purpose in that group. But if your goal is to continuously meet different people with different backgrounds, you will want to save time and energy for other activities, as well. I've noticed that the longer one plays a sport or participates in the same activity, the more people he or she knows, but the less diverse his or her circle of friends becomes. Conversations or relationships in these circles may be based entirely on the activity. If you're looking for a deeper exchange, you may want to be careful to keep other options open for meeting people.

TAKEAWAYS:

- Travel around the world by yourself. Experiencing other cultures will open up your mind to new ways of living, and offer you opportunities to make new friends.

- Take dance lessons—any kind! It's a natural way to meet other people.

- Be careful to not get so involved in one group or activity that you miss out on meeting people with different backgrounds and interests. Keep time available for other activities as well.

Chapter 14

STEP ELEVEN: TEAM NO SLEEP

Five years ago, I had never heard of the slogan, "Team No Sleep." I thought, what does that mean? How do you not sleep? But once I started living the lifestyle, I embraced the term and became its poster child. Living the "Team No Sleep" lifestyle means that I am living life to the fullest every single day. I go out, meet people, work, network, work out, meet more people and do it again the next day. Is it exhausting? Occasionally. Does it require a lot of energy? Absolutely. But I have found this lifestyle to be incredibly worth it.

There is so much we can do in this lifetime—why spend time sitting on a couch watching TV or playing video games, when we could be doing a million other things? If the former is your lifestyle, I recommend you start doing something different every single day. Make it a point to talk to new people or to try out a new activity. You can't make new friends from your living room.

You may need to get over some mental barriers that we tell ourselves way too often: "I can't," "I'm too tired," "There's not enough time in a day to do that..." But all you need to do is consider your priorities. If you really want to make new friends, you'll find the time to get out there. Nothing will change unless you want it to change. You have to have the desire, the drive, the fire to make it happen. And you must accept that nothing will fall into your lap; you have to take action.

How do you join "Team No Sleep?" Are there tryouts? Not necessarily. Many people have tried to join the team and many have failed. It's not for the faint of heart. The main requirement is energy – you'll need a lot of positive energy to remain on the team. You're probably thinking, doesn't energy require sleep? That is partially true. There are some days where you need more sleep than others, but people often psyche themselves out before they even try to join the team: "I need nine hours of sleep. I can't function on that little of sleep, it's impossible." FALSE! It's impossible because you just said it is.

It does take training to get your body and mind ready to go on little sleep. The first trick to staying out late and making it into work on time the next day is to not drink more than two or three drinks. Don't try to impress people by how much you can drink – if your friends are real friends, they could care less how much you drink. The next trick is to train your body and mind over time that you don't need seven or eight or nine hours of sleep. Tell yourself that five or six will do just fine, and like magic, that's what you'll get. Imagine how many more things you can do in a day with those extra one to two hours! In a year, you will have had over 500 hours more to do whatever you want to do in your life.

For me, I realized that sleep wasn't a necessity when I was jet-setting across the globe, flying fifteen hours nonstop to foreign countries. You've heard of jet lag, right? I don't believe in it. It's a myth. If you tell your body and mind that you're on whatever time it is where you land, then poof! Watch your body adjust. The shift becomes nothing. You just have to truly believe it. If you tell yourself that you're going to get jet lag, you're going to be in sleep deprivation mode until who knows when.

Have you ever felt lethargic while at home, but you decided to go out and meet up with your friends anyway? How did you feel after that? You probably felt great, right? Moving around and being social gave you that extra shot of energy. The trick is to keep on moving.

NO SNOOZE ALLOWED

You may have heard that by sleeping less, you may eventually cut away five years of your life. But even if that is true, I'd rather have one hell of a time in my twenties and thirties and live to be 95 instead of 100 years old. These are the days you'll remember—the days where you're young, wild, and free. There is no better time to stay out late, get a little crazy, and experience life while you're healthy.

Start a training regimen to get on a six or seven hours of sleep per night rotation, versus however much you're sleeping now. And for your own sake, put your alarm far away from your bed so you are forced to get out of bed in the morning. If your alarm is right next to your bed, it's too easy to hit the snooze. And lastly, stop wasting time binge-watching TV shows. Who cares if you're not up to date on the latest shows? The conversations you have with your friends shouldn't all center on TV shows or movies anyway. We weren't meant to be sedentary – we have two legs because we're supposed to be moving and shaking!

DON'T WORK TOO MUCH

One of my favorite mantras is, "If you're not having fun, then it's time to stop what you're doing and find something else to do with your time." This mantra can be applied to multiple situations, whether it's for work or for play. Chasing fun is a lost art. Remember when you were a kid and didn't have a worry in the world? What did you care about? Hanging out with your friends and having fun, right? Who says you can't do that now?

When you're older and looking back on your life, work will be an afterthought. The trips and crazy things you did will be what you remember. So what's the point of focusing so much time on work? Don't fall into the rat race trap of working eighty hours a week for "the man." It's just not worth it. I'd choose to live a life well-lived with great friends over being wealthy and having zero friends and no great experiences. Wouldn't you?

Don't get confused—money doesn't buy happiness, it definitely doesn't buy your friends, and it's not guaranteed to buy you fun. Those things are up to you. Why worry about money? If you leave this world tomorrow, you can't take it with you.

You can have great experiences regardless of how much cash you have in your pocket. Experiences are really about the people. Going to the beach is free. Having a picnic doesn't cost much (you were going to buy food anyway). Having people over for a game night doesn't cost anything. Think outside of the box to bring your friends together and have fun—don't assume you can't have fun because you don't have "enough" money.

TAKEAWAYS:

- Train your mind and train your body to be able to function on less sleep and pack more enjoyment into your life.

- Chase fun. Find creative ways to have fun, just as you did when you were a child.

- You don't have to spend money in order to have great experiences.

Chapter 15

STEP TWELVE: JUST SAY "YES"

When you just say "yes"...to nearly everything...amazing things happen! There are certain things I do say no to; I'm not too keen on bungee jumping, nor eating bugs, nor traveling to certain places where I would fear for my life (say the death road in Bolivia). However, to meet people, make friends, and get connected wherever you are, just say "yes." Sure, you may be put in uncomfortable situations, but you never know until you try things once, right?

Make yourself available to anything that comes your way. Be on your toes, ready to go, and be open to being spontaneous. Don't think about it—just do it! When someone invites you to something that you've never heard of, seem to have no interest in, and no desire to go to, forget all that—just go! When you start hanging in circles outside of your own, you will meet more people and have the most diverse conversations. People will ask you, "How do you know so many people?"

Because you just say "yes" to everything that comes your way!

Once upon a time here in Tampa, I saw an invitation to a women's networking event through the chamber of commerce called Pearls of Wisdom. It didn't say it was limited to women, but that was the general impression of the event. There was a woman keynote speaker, and they were talking about women's empowerment. Why would I ever want to go to such an event? Easy—because I knew I would be severely outnumbered by women, and it would be an easy conversation starter since I would be one of the few men there (or as it turned out, the only man).

Don't be afraid to put yourself out there. Stand out from the crowd. Put yourself in a situation that causes people to start talking to you. How awesome is it when you don't have to do the heavy lifting? When people come talk to you and start a conversation, it saves you time and energy, and you know they're interested in what you have to say because they approached you. However, it's then on you to engage them back and turn the conversation into something worthwhile.

At that women's event, I proved myself a worthwhile counterpart, made a number of new friends, and then started getting invited to other women's events. Now it's become routine for me to hang out with thirty, forty, or fifty women at various events because I'm friends with at least half of the room. They treat me just like any of the women there. Now, I'm not sure if that's a positive or negative thing, but I treat it as positive because it's always much better to have a team of women working on your side than against you.

You never know what's going to happen when you say "yes." It's part of the adventure, the mystique. Hanging out with new people in new places, doing things you'd never dream of doing. How exciting is that?

One of my favorite things to do at new places is to sit and talk to strangers. I don't necessarily mean out on the street or at a bar, but rather at parties, sporting events, etc. How are you going to meet new people and make new friends if you only associate with the five friends you came with? If you have the opportunity to sit down next to someone you don't know - do it! Just say "yes."

...BUT PROCEED WITH CAUTION

Now there is one caveat I'll add here. There are people in my life who I love dearly and who are my good friends—but I would never say "yes" to traveling with them! I know who I am, what I like to do, and who I can tolerate in certain situations. My patience runs very thin when I travel; if I'm going backpacking with you in South America, you best not be bringing three suitcases, one of which is just for shoes.

When making travel plans, you have to know your friends. Know what they like, know who they are, know their quirks. Developing this knowledge takes time; you have to have experiences together. Maybe you need to take a few weekend excursions to see how that person is while traveling. I also like to see how my friends treat other people; that's a very solid way to judge their character. Also, who do your friends hang out with? Who people keep as friends says a lot about who they are, too.

LEAVE SPACE FOR SPONTANEITY

While traveling through South America, I came across two women who were very nice, down-to-earth girls from Canada. They were well traveled, well educated, and...they knew what they were doing. They had their whole itinerary planned out, long before they arrived in Brazil. They did the research, they "knew" the best spots to visit, which tour groups to join and so on. But what they didn't leave open was the option to say "yes" to any invitations that unexpectedly came their way. "Hey, we're going to have a beach barbeque, you guys should come!... Oh, you can't because you've already planned to go to a soccer game."

Trust me, I'm all for planning—it's how I run my life every day. I have to have a plan, or else nothing gets accomplished. However, I leave my plan open for suggestions, as I like to say. If people invite me to something, or if I hear of a great event I didn't know about before, I move my schedule around to make it happen.

LIVE WITH NO REGRETS

If you had thirty days to live, how would you live them? You've likely heard the phrase, "Live like there's no tomorrow." You may not want to get that extreme, but it is good to live life to the fullest every single day. Another mantra of mine is, "No regrets." I want to go to sleep every night knowing that I did the best I could that day and that I have zero regrets. When you have this feeling at the end of the day, it makes falling asleep 100 times easier because you have nothing to look back on that needs to be addressed for tomorrow.

When given the opportunity to do something, I ask myself, "How will I feel if I say no?" If I'm unsure, then I know it's probably not a good decision to say no. If I know that an opportunity only happens once every so often, then there's a 90% chance I will do whatever I was on the fence about. Life is all about opportunity— the opportunity to do something with your life, to take a chance, to explore, to go on an adventure and have an experience. In the end, we'll look back on our lives and remember the experiences we had and the people we met along the way.

We all have fears. "No regrets" means facing your fears and overcoming them. At one time, I didn't really care to speak in front of people. However, I started getting routinely invited to speak to groups and I'd just say "yes." I didn't leave myself time to think about it.

It's much more fun to live a life full of yes's than one full of no's. When you say no, you're only giving into your fears and what you can't accomplish. Tell yourself you can do anything you set your mind to, take a deep breath, and go. This way, you can look back on your life and be proud of everything you accomplished—every door you kicked down, every crazy adventure you went on. It's those experiences that will shape you for the rest of your life.

The same can be said about relationships as well—some are good, some are bad, some blow up in your face. However, you don't know until you try and if it doesn't work out, remind yourself of this phrase: "No regrets." Learn from your mistakes and move on.

The greatest risk we face is not doing anything at all. Everything we do in life involves some level of risk. When you get in your car and go to work, you're taking a risk that you won't get into an accident. When you bite into a sandwich from a restaurant, you're taking a risk that the food was prepared properly. When you go for a run, you take a risk that your knees won't give out. We deal with these risks and have become so accustomed to them that we write them off as just our daily routine. But what we don't realize is that the biggest risk of all is sitting there idle, and doing nothing.

Doing nothing is taking the risk that your life is just going to pass you by. One day you'll wake up and be eighty-five years old, and you'll wonder where the hell your life went.

How much time are you going to be here—to make an impact, to leave a legacy, to make people remember you? And remember—

the bigger the risk, the bigger the reward. If you're sitting there on the sidelines, your chances of a big reward are slim to none.

TAKEAWAYS:

- Make yourself available to anything that comes your way. Don't be afraid to be spontaneous.

- Take the opportunity to sit and talk to strangers—at a park bench, on the bus, in line for coffee.

- Live each day to the fullest, so when you go to bed at night, you have no regrets.

Chapter 16

STEP THIRTEEN: CHANGE YOUR ROUTINES

We all have routines that we follow every day and every week. Some routines we might not even notice: How we go to bed, what we eat for breakfast, the first thing we do when we go to work, grabbing take out from the same pizza place every Friday night. Why do we like routines so much? Because they're safe. They're comfortable. They're known. They're broken in like an old pair of shoes.

It's not easy to toss out that pair of shoes because they're just so comfortable. Buying a new pair of shoes brings up a lot of unknowns: They fit in the store, but how are they going to fit when I wear them every day? Will they make my feet hurt? Can I go dancing in them? Do they look as good as my previous pair?

The same can be said for making friends. It's so much easier spending the weekend with one or two friends, doing the same thing, going to the same bars, the same restaurants, the same activities. But how are you going to make new friends if you keep following the same routines? You have to go out and explore and be adventurous. Check out a new part of the city. Try a new sport or a new activity.

For all of the people reading this who are telling themselves, "I can't," get rid of that statement from your vocabulary and replace it with, "I will." I will go down to that sports league and sign up for intramural basketball. I will go to that book club at the civic center. I will volunteer this weekend at the homeless shelter. There are a million things to do—you just have to pick a handful and stick with them.

ROUTINES YOU DO NEED TO KEEP

On the flip side, I will say that some routines are good and do in fact serve a purpose. To be a good friend you must be loyal, committed and dedicated. If you're going to join a sports team, you need to be an active participant for the entire season and not disappear midway through. The same goes for any organization; if you sign up to volunteer, you need to follow through with your commitment and make it a routine for however long you signed up for.

Aside from being steadfast and dedicated, routines are also good because people will know where to find you. If you go to the gym on Monday, Wednesday, and Friday mornings at 6 a.m., you'll most likely start making friends with others who follow the same routine. If you volunteer at the soup kitchen on Thursday nights, you'll start making friends with others who are there at the same time.

Life is about balance. You have to have both the yin and the yang. Be spontaneous, but keep a routine for certain things.

There's also a fine line about becoming too boring or too predictable, which is the downside of routines. If you eat the same breakfast every day, do the same workout every other day, and go to the same bar every Saturday night, life becomes stale. You are not a robot, so don't get caught in the habit of building your life around routines. Mix it up and do both, and after a certain period of time exchange your routines for some new routines.

Go out and join some new organizations and see what you think. And don't judge your experience based on one time, i.e. "it just wasn't my crowd." How do you know? Just by going one time and staying there for thirty minutes? Give it another try, and see if it gets better.

DIVERSITY IS KEY

If you insert yourself into fifteen different groups, you're going to have the most diverse group of friends, because you have your hands in a multitude of areas.

If I were to have stayed in the beach volleyball scene, then I would have limited myself to that small segment of people and the friends of friends who are all in that scene. Over time, however, that scene would have become old. There are thousands of other people who live around you who you could be friends with too, even if you have to drive or take a train to the next biggest city in order to meet them.

Make the extra effort and try a number of groups out to see what best fits you. You never know until you try. You may think that the cooking class down the street would be lame, but maybe you show up and meet a number of other fun people just like you. Don't stop yourself with negative thoughts before you leave your house.

DITCH THE TECHNOLOGY ROUTINE

Making friends takes time, effort, and the ability to actually care about other people. As we've become more reliant on technology, we've all become lazier, myself included. Do you remember the days where you had to actually read a map and ask for directions if you got lost? There weren't any GPS devices that could guide you to your destination. Or how about when you went out to a bar and met a cute girl; in order to get her number, you had to ask the bartender for a pen and a napkin so you could write it down? Seems crazy right?

It wasn't that long ago—not even twenty years. Back then we all had to be a bit more accountable for our actions. If I told my friends I was going to be there at 7 p.m., I better be there at 7 p.m., because I didn't have a cell phone and there was no way to let them know otherwise. If I wanted to ask a girl out, I actually had to call her (on her landline!). Can you believe that? A phone call to ask someone out? Sounds like so much effort, but back then it was just what you did and everything turned out all right.

For thousands of years, we as humans have craved interaction with each other. Nothing has changed over time—communication has just migrated over to less intimate ways to interact, via texting and apps. Technology has diminished our ability to be social like we once were. I'm sure you see it every day—people out on dates who are on their cell phones because they forgot what it's like to have a real face-to-face conversation.

Go out there and start having face-to-face, REAL conversations with people that are more than just surface level conversations about the weather, sports, work, or other such things. Ask deeper level questions—ones which show you really care about the other person and that you are genuinely interested in what they have to say.

TAKEAWAYS

- Consider the routines you currently have. Look for opportunities to break them.

- Set a new routine—whether it be joining an intramural sport or volunteering on a regular basis. Honor your commitment, but then look for new routines to replace that one again.

- Remember, there was a time when smartphones didn't exist. Act like they don't on occasion—call someone instead of text, and have an entire evening out with a friend where you don't even check your phone once.

Chapter 17

STEP FOURTEEN: FIND YOUR PURPOSE, FOLLOW YOUR PASSION

NEVER STOP ASKING WHY

How often do you hear the phrase "follow your passion"? Does answering that one question give you the meaning of life? Doubtful. Having passion is great; it's determining what to do with your passion and matching it with your purpose in life that will get you to where you want to be. By doing so, you're going to meet some great people along the way.

But how do you even start this process? I wish there was a simple formula to determine someone's purpose in life. I don't know about you, but I've asked myself these questions many times: Why am I here? What am I doing with my life? Where is my life going?

Do these questions have easy answers? Heck no! If they were easy to answer then we'd all be living in bliss, and there wouldn't be half as many problems in the world. It took me more than thirty years to figure out my "why." Maybe you're lucky and it won't take you as long as it took me, or maybe you won't figure it out until you're fifty. In the end, it doesn't really matter; as long as you're looking for a deeper purpose in life, you'll get there. Just be patient.

The main factor is to keep asking "why?" Everywhere you go, every person you meet—ask why. Why did I meet this person? Why should I go to that event? Why did this happen to me? Think back to when you were a little kid. How many times did you ask "why?" You probably drove your parents nuts just like any other kid. There is no reason to stop being curious. The older we get, the more curious you should become because you're going to have much more knowledge at hand. Question everything and critically consider why things are happening. We're all "so busy" living our lives that we forget to ask "why" and therefore we overlook certain aspects of our life that have real meaning.

You never know when your "why" will come to you. My "why" came to me after trying many unsatisfying jobs back in Indianapolis and finally just packing up my bags and moving 1,000 miles to the south, where I knew one person. I asked myself why am I here? Why the hell did I pack up my bags at thirty years old and move to Florida? Am I retiring? Am I supposed to be playing golf three days a week? Am I supposed to sign up for the shuffleboard league?

Eventually, I came to my real "why": I was here to start a business— something that wasn't even on my mind when I first moved to Florida. That's the brilliant thing in life. You have to keep the faith that things will work themselves out and that you're moving forward in life because that is the only direction to go.

My friend Kate, for example, created a charity that helps people who have been domestically abused. That cause is near and dear to her heart, and helping people who have suffered abuse makes her happy. Now, she has a following in multiple cities. When you find that cause that makes you happy, you'll be amazed by what will happen next.

CASE STUDY: KATE

I cringe when I hear the word "passion" because I remember all the times I would rack my brain trying to "find my passion" only to feel empty, uninspired, and bitter towards those that seemed to effortlessly have found theirs.

But, I am aware that some people feel the same way when I tell them my story. When I was twenty-six years old, I founded a nonprofit organization that uses yoga to support and empower survivors and raises awareness about domestic violence, sexual assault, and trauma. It was a big undertaking, mostly because I had no idea what I was doing or how I would take this on. I did, however, know *why* I wanted to do this, and that I needed to go down this road.

When I was sixteen years old I met a boy who would end up being my first abuser. When I was twenty-three, I met my second abuser. I would have never guessed that both men that seemed so well-intentioned would end up being the ones that hurt me the most.

These two experiences, however, were the most obvious ones that connected me to my purpose. There were many more connections to come. Uncovering them wasn't always easy, but as Elizabeth Gilbert says in her book *Big Magic*, "if you can let go of 'passion' and follow your curiosity, your curiosity just might *lead* you to your passion."

Starting Purple Dot Yoga Project was more than a way to give back to the domestic violence community. I wanted to make ALL people understand that we are all suffering, or have suffered. At the essence of our being we really just want people to see us, to hear us, to feel with us.

Purple Dot Yoga Project is my gift to the world. I was able to uncover this gift by paying attention to what occurred in my life and being curious to the lessons those experiences had for me.

Pay attention. When you find something that makes you wonder, follow it diligently. Follow it with revere, with honor, and with the understanding that this will lead you to your purpose. Your purpose lies within you, waiting to be uncovered. It's not something that needs to be found, it already belongs to you.

My friend Brianna has a similar story. She found her "why" through various jobs in the healthcare field. After so many years of working for others, she decided it was time to do her own thing and she took the leap of faith to start her own recruiting company. Her purpose was to help other people get jobs and also to fill a niche market that didn't have much competition.

She could have taken the safer route and worked at a company for many years, but she trusted her gut and her intuition to make that move. She knew she had to lay it on the line and take that risk, and she has never looked back.

LIVE A PURPOSEFUL LIFE

Why are you here? What is your mission in life? How do you want to be remembered? When you're eighty-five years old looking back on your life, what is going to be your legacy? These are the questions I want you to think about long and hard. That is the purpose of this book—I want you to get out there and LIVE! I'm not telling you to quit your job or take any drastic steps.... yet. But do seriously consider, what are you doing with your life? Everyone can go through life, work a job, do the "same ol', same ol'." But are you everyone? Be someone who makes a difference. Touch somebody's life in a way that they'll never forget. Live a purposeful life.

Have you ever traveled abroad to see how people in different countries live their lives? Imagine you're going to Paris, where love is in the air and people work thirty-five hours a week. Sounds too good to be true, right? Well, it is not—it really does happen. And it's not just France, there are plenty of other countries who put work-life balance at the top of the list for employee benefits; they get six to eight weeks of paid vacation, plus government and bank holidays! And somehow they still manage to get things done during the day and live a full life.

People in the U.S. have been brainwashed into following what "Corporate America" needs us to do—work over fifty hours a week. We'll receive a two-week paid vacation if we're lucky enough to actually take off work without getting so behind in our workload that we don't even want to take a vacation. It's a vicious cycle, and that kind of job is seriously going to kill you—whether mentally or physically. It's time to leave that job behind and find your real purpose in life.

Now is the time. If the place you're at isn't where you want to be, move! If now is not the right time, when is the right time going to be? There never is a "right" time. If there was, it would be easy to figure out when to make a move. You have to find the courage to make some tough decisions now.

WHAT ARE YOU PASSIONATE ABOUT?

Are you passionate about animals? A sports team? Helping people? Working out? Traveling? These are all great things you can definitely be passion about, but in the larger picture of life, what does it really matter? If I'm passionate about helping people, how can I turn that into a viable business? If I'm passionate about animals, what career path can I take if I have zero desire to be a veterinarian?

We can all be passionate about a variety of items, but the odds of me quitting my job to follow my passion are probably pretty slim because it's tough to make a living solely based on what I'm passionate about. I'm passionate about tennis—it's one of the main reasons I moved to Florida, so I could play year-round. But I'm not good enough to be a tennis pro, so I knew my purpose had to be something else.

I prefer to trade the word "passionate" for "enjoy." I really enjoy playing tennis. I really enjoy spending time with my dog. I really enjoy volunteering. Doesn't that sound better? I think the term passion has become too much of a cliché and that it's used out of context way too often.

So if the word "passion" trips you up, just ask yourself, what do you enjoy? What motivates you to get out of bed in the morning? When you figure that question out, you'll be on the right path to where you need to go. If you have a hard time getting out of bed in the morning, then it's probably time to reevaluate your life and start making those tough decisions we talked about.

IT'S UP TO YOU

When you do find your purpose, you're going to uncover a treasure trove of other people who most likely will have similar interests as you. When you're in the same field, it's much easier to bounce ideas of other like-minded people. So brace yourself—because the day you figure this out will be the day your life changes forever, in a good way! The light bulb will go off and you'll have that moment of clarity as to why you are here and what your mission in life is. You'll stop worrying about money and focus on your purpose because that's what matters above all else.

And in regards to money—if you're focusing on money, then you didn't find your purpose. Your purpose is above money. Money cannot sustain your drive over time and it certainly won't get you to wherever you want to go in life. Life is about chasing your dreams. Taking a stab at the unknown. Taking risks. If you want something to happen, you have to make it happen. It's up to you and no one else. You have to hold yourself accountable and if you can't, find a friend or family member to hold your feet to the fire.

TAKEAWAYS:

- Be very curious in life. Ask "why?" about everything.

- You must plan today for tomorrow, or else you're going to remain in the status quo doing the same thing over and over.

- Relax—it takes time to find your purpose.

Chapter 18

STEP FIFTEEN: TREAT OTHERS LIKE YOU'D LIKE TO BE TREATED

My experience studying abroad in Manchester, England taught me a lesson I carry with me today. I was a bright-eyed, twenty-year-old Midwesterner. I had never left the country so I figured what better way to embark on a journey abroad than to study in England, because hey, they speak English, right? Well, in their own manner. It was an experience I never anticipated and it changed my life forever.

When I first arrived at the university, I was not at all welcomed by my flatmates—seven British students who already had their sets of friends loosely gave me a hello when I walked in the room. To move to another country and try to blend in, but still keep your identity, is hard to do. To not feel welcomed when I arrived was like adding salt to an open wound.

I took that experience back with me and I use it as inspiration to help others. If I'm hosting my own event or attending another, I want to ensure people have a feeling of being welcomed and accepted. Part of what I do today through my company New Town Connections is exactly that—helping people who are new in town to get acclimated to the city and to make new friends.

Through my experiences abroad, not just in England but other places I've lived and traveled, I want to make sure everyone I meet is happy, well-connected, and has friends. Having real friends is invaluable. You cannot put a price tag on what it means to have a group of friends or best friends. I know there are a lot of lonely people out there, so why not help them out? Invite them to an event. Make them part of the group. It's not much fun living on an island by yourself; as humans, we are all very social creatures who like to live life in community. I encourage and challenge you to go out and be that person who makes others feel welcome— all it takes is an invite. They might end up becoming great friends of yours as a result.

Jen is my networking counterpart. Everywhere I go to network, she is there. If you were looking to find Miss Congeniality, she is it. She too has the gift of energy and warmth. Wherever she goes, so knows no stranger. She also moved to Florida from the north and had to start at ground zero, but because of all her great assets, she increased her network by thousands. If you saw her out in public today you would guess that she has been in Florida for her entire life.

CASE STUDY: JEN

I sincerely enjoy meeting new people. Whether it is through my business network, my neighborhood or in my social circles, meeting new people keeps my life interesting and helps me grow as a person. Recognizing this, I walk into every room with an open mind, excited about meeting someone new.

While no one wants to waste their time or feel unwelcome, some people aren't comfortable networking or talking with strangers. That's where I step in and stand out. I understand that not everyone is comfortable walking up to new people, so I enjoy playing that role. If I spot someone in the room standing alone I will make a point to introduce myself, get to know them, and introduce them to others.

I always greet people with a smile and a genuine interest in learning about them. When I meet new people I focus on learning what they are interested in and what they want to take away from that particular event or gathering. I use this insight to introduce them to other people they might find interesting. Before making that introduction I will explain to them why I think they should meet a particular person: As a business contact, a potential date, or simply to make a new friend in town. Making that introduction shows that I listened to them and acted in their best interest, which also helps build our relationship.

There are many ways someone can stand out in a room, both good and bad. I enjoy standing out as someone who helps make connections for others and ensuring everyone feels included.

WALK IN SOMEONE ELSE'S SHOES

To be a great friend you need to be there for each other, show empathy and know what it's like to walk in each other's shoes. Until you do so, at times you may find it hard to relate to some of your friends. It's your job as a friend to be there in the good times and the bad. Real friends are there for you when things get tough, to offer that shoulder to lean on and an ear to listen to whatever's going on. It's easy being a friend when you're all having fun; it's difficult when you have to be there when things go south—at times like this, you can't just disappear.

I like to envision myself in someone else's shoes before I open up my mouth and say something. There's a saying, "Everyone is fighting their own battle, so don't be quick to draw conclusions." People have bad days, good days, and other days where they just go through the motions. We're all human, and we all need to treat each other with dignity, respect, and humility. Being nice doesn't cost anything.

It's not hard to start a conversation with someone. Just ask, "How's your day going?" They could reply with a quick "fine" or it could turn into a very elaborate answer that dumps everything onto you. That's probably not what you bargained for, but it is something worth preparing for. To be human is to show that you do have a heart and you do care. Good friends are empathetic and pick up on things that are off—the longer you're friends with someone, the more you know when things don't seem the same. That's when you start asking questions because you do care. That extra effort is what separates a good friend from a best friend.

Have you ever been having a bad day, then either your spouse or a friend did something for you that turned your day around? Maybe they ordered your favorite meal for dinner, or they sent over your favorite flowers. They did these things because they anticipated what would brighten up your day. Imagine if you did the same for some of your friends from time to time. If you want to have real friendships that are more than just surface level chatter, I highly recommend you put yourself in someone else's shoes and then start to anticipate what they need.

Life is like a game of chess. If you want to stand out from the crowd, you want to be thinking at least two to four moves ahead. Don't focus so much on immediate needs, because anyone else can do that. These are the little things that you can do to make a killer impression with people. And the best part is it doesn't even have to be something big or out of the ordinary.

How great would it be if you could read someone's mind? You could do something for them that would be exactly what they were thinking or wanting! Being on the same wavelength as another person, knowing how they think, what they want, and being able to get a step ahead of them involves anticipation. Anticipation comes from a variety of angles, which can be broken down into body language, the ability to listen and listen carefully, paying attention to detail, remembering random bits of information, and making an effort.

What's important to others may not be important to you, so the hard work here is getting outside of your own comfort zone and putting others' needs in front of your own. The act of being selfless is another good step toward connecting with other people. When you put other people first, they will notice and appreciate that you're being unselfish, which will go a long way toward making friends. At the end of the day, you want others to remember you for being a caring person who took care of your friends first over your own needs.

In life, we all have our day to day struggles. Most of the time, we don't know what people are going through because of various reasons. As such, I always think about this question: Who am I to judge? If I just met you at an event and you're having an off day for whatever reason, it's not my place to judge you as being a rude person with zero personality. I have no idea what the rest of your day was like, so I should not worry about it and move along with my evening.

You can't get hung up on the little things and you definitely can't please everyone. How many times have you met someone, pre-judged them, and then found out later that you were totally wrong on your initial assessment? It happens all the time. People judge each other for what they wear, the car they drive, the job they have, where they live, who they hang around, how much money they make and so on. Does any of that really matter in the bigger scheme of things? Nope! None of it matters. The only thing that truly matters is who you are and if you're happy. And you're the only person who gets to decide if you're happy or not.

BE A TEAM PLAYER

In life, you want to be a team player just as you would be expected to be on a sports team or debate team or any other kind of team. Help introduce people to each other at events. Volunteer to clean up afterward. Make your presence known. Showing up to an event is one thing—making a lasting impression is a whole other story.

Good things happen to people who dedicate themselves to others, to causes, and to people in general. However, when you sacrifice your time and yourself for others, just make sure it's for the right reasons and that you're not getting taken advantage of. It should be your call to sacrifice, not others forcing you into a situation where you're making unwanted sacrifices.

Being on sports teams helped me learn how to compete, how to socialize with others I had nothing in common with outside of the sport, how to get coached, how to be disciplined, how to earn respect from other players, and how to work hard. What you learn while on any team can be applied in life. And don't think this just applies to sports teams—you can be on any team, whether that's a debate team, political team, trivia team, or a team of volunteers. As long as you're with others working toward a common goal, I would define that as a team.

And when you're on a team, there really is no other way but to work together, otherwise, you're going to fail. That's why communication skills are so critical. If you're not communicating effectively you won't be well-liked, and it's going to be hard for others to want to work with you. You may soon become isolated from the rest of the group.

Teams with one star player never make it very far. The star player is either relied upon too much, or the star player doesn't live up to expectations. Teams that have an equal balance of good players are the ones who always go further than the rest. If you can surround yourself with a team of good friends, you'll go farther than you would if you only had one or two best friends that you have to rely on for most of your social outings.

WORDS OF CAUTION

Don't spend time helping those who don't want to be helped. Yes, you should help other people, but I do have to make one caveat to that—you can't always help people who don't want to be helped. When you get sucked into their realm before you know it you've wasted a vast amount of your time on someone who never wanted to be helped in the first place. How do you avoid this rabbit hole? Sometimes we get too eager to help everyone because we all think they're looking for it. So take a step back, assess the situation and see if the person you're trying to help is really looking for help or if you're just sticking your nose where it doesn't belong.

I usually give people a few chances to test the waters and see if they really want my help. If not, no harm no foul, I move on and life goes on. Older people, in particular, most likely will have a harder time accepting help because they're typically set in their ways. Don't get offended if they tell you they don't need your help. Just smile, nod your head, and move along.

TAKEAWAYS:

- Look for opportunities to make others feel welcomed and engaged—if you're at an event and you see someone by themselves, introduce him or her to others.

- Don't make judgments about someone you only met once—you never know what they've gone through that day.

- Anticipate what your friends might need before they need to ask for it.

Chapter 19

STEP SIXTEEN: LOVE IS ALL YOU NEED

Imagine a world where everyone loved more and hated less. That's my utopia. I want to live somewhere that embraces love and makes people feel special and appreciated. Too often today people are kicked to the curb for a variety of reasons. It's too easy to be a bully and make fun of other people.

It may seem hard to tell people you love them, but it's really not. You just have to feel it and believe it when you say it. The impact you have when you do this is far greater than what you think. We've often been told that you can only love so many people at any given time—your family, your spouse, and maybe a best friend. Don't believe it! You can love as many people as you want. It's up to you. I have many friends who I love dearly and I tell them that every time I see them; I look them in the eye and say, "I love you." How many of your friends do that to you? Or how often do you do this to your friends? Start doing it today. Of course, you don't have to say it to everyone, but do say it to the people you truly care for and see what their reaction is. Some people get it and they'll say, "I love you too," and others will just say, "Thanks," which is fine.

It's not about what you get back in return, it's about what you put out. How often do you hear or see in the news stories about people who pass away before their time and their friends and family say, "I wish I could have said goodbye?" Or, "I wish I could have told them how much I loved them?" Don't be that person. We all have feelings—there's nothing wrong with sharing them. Time doesn't slow down for anyone and you'll only regret not telling people you love them when you had the chance.

WHAT IS LOVE?

What is love? Is it just a feeling? Does is take weeks, months, or years to attain? Is love at first sight a real thing? It depends on what you believe. I love many friends who I've only known a short period of time. If I'm in a relationship, that's a different story. When you feel a spark between you and someone else, it is magic. To me, love is the chemistry, the conversation, the intangible things you feel when you're around that person. It's almost as if they have an aura surrounding them. That's love, at least in my world.

When it comes to relationships, I definitely do not jump in that boat of saying "I love you" after the first three dates (don't be that person!). I use a similar frame of mind for my friends. I say "I love you" to them usually after a few months and after hanging out with them on multiple occasions.

You have to get to know a person on a real level—know who they are, what they like, what they aspire to be, and take it from there. Using the "love" word has to remain special and not just feel like any other word in the dictionary. It's not a football and shouldn't be tossed around lightly.

Real friendships are made of love—that feeling that you know the other person will be there for you through thick and thin. When you hug them, touch them, or are just around them you can feel it. There's no other way to describe it. And when you're giving off that sensation and feeling of love, others will feel it as well.

It is worth mentioning that there are different levels of love. You don't have to love everyone equally—in fact, it's quite the opposite. Some people you will love a little, some in the middle, and some you will love a lot. The longer you are friends with someone, the deeper that love will become.

LOVE YOURSELF FIRST

Don't forget, however, that you also must love yourself. Plain and simple. How can you love others if you're not happy with yourself? Take everything that's already been mentioned and apply it to yourself. Do the things in life that you want to do, and then take that newly acquired happiness and share it with others.

TAKEAWAYS:

- Love often—and don't be afraid to tell your loved ones how you feel about them.

- The longer you get to know someone, the deeper the love will grow.

- It's not about what you get back in return, it's about what you put out.

Chapter 20

STEP SEVENTEEN: NO EXCUSES

How often have you used an excuse to not go out? "I'm too busy." "I'm too tired." "I have too much work to do." "I can't." "My dog is sick." "I have to hang out with my significant other." All sound legitimate, but if you want to make friends you need to stop making excuses and just go out.

Here in America, most of us work longer hours than the rest of the world, which doesn't leave much time to sleep, eat, and see your family or friends, right? Actually, wrong! We make time for what's important to us. By just saying those excuse statements, you make them come true. Why don't you flip those sayings around and say, "I am free" or "I would love to." You have to shift your mind over to more positive thinking in order to get away from those excuses.

YOUR WORD IS YOUR REALITY

To help with this you need to change up your vocabulary. Eliminate the word "busy" right now. When someone asks how you have been, don't say "busy." What does that word even mean? We're all busy. Instead, start saying, "I can" or, "I am" and stop using "I can't," "I'll try," or "Maybe." People like definitive answers in addition to positive answers. The more you say, "I'm too busy" or "I can't," the fewer people will invite you out, and sooner or later the invites will stop coming and your wish will become a reality.

Commit to something please, for the sake of everyone. Just make a decision and stick with it. You're only as good as your word, and once you break your word, people will remember that and your trust goes out the window. And if you can't be trusted, what kind of friend are you?

TAKE INITIATIVE

Another common excuse I hear is, "No one invites me out." Who says you can't be the one inviting people out? If you want to do something, or go somewhere, or see anything, make it happen. Don't wait for others to make plans. Invite other people! And if you don't know anyone, go make some friends through one of the various ways mentioned in this book.

The more good energy vibes you put out there, the more will come back to you tenfold. Start inviting people to anything— coffee, brunch, lunch, happy hour, sports games, festivals, the beach, hiking, runs, the movies, anything! There are literally hundreds of activities to choose from depending on where you live and the weather. Surely you can find a few that suit what you like and invite others to come along.

People like to be invited to things, and with technology, it's easy! You can shoot out a text to ten people in a matter of a couple minutes. The more of an effort you make, the more your friends will appreciate you and the more things you're going to get invited to. Don't wait for life to happen—make it happen, and start today!

YOU CAN NEVER HAVE "ENOUGH" FRIENDS

I am always amused when I hear people say, "I have enough friends, I don't need any more." These people tend to be short-sighted and have a rosy view as to how friendships and relationships work. I'm always an optimist, but I do like to have secondary options as you never know when friends get better opportunities and move away or move on with their life.

Things change and you need to be prepared for life to happen, whether because of your own circumstances or your friends' circumstances. Over time, I've learned that most friends cycle in and cycle out ever two to four years. You have your core group of friends or best friends who have maybe been around beyond that, but I would venture to say that's probably less than five people.

Your other friends who are in the secondary tier churn over pretty often due to a variety of reasons. This continues to happen to me all the time; I hang out with one group of friends for a couple of years and then I find a different group of friends to hang out with for a couple years and the cycle keeps repeating. That pattern may be a result of my own doing, as I love variety. I like to have my hands in multiple areas, whether that's through sports, through charities, through networking groups, through universities, through church, or whatever else you can think of.

To me, you can never have enough friends. To believe otherwise is a short-sighted approach and will only do harm to you down the road. Allow more friends into your life, because you never know who you're going to meet and what they're going to lead you to.

STAY DRIVEN

What separates most successful people from others? Drive. Some people have the work ethic to keep on going when things look dim, while others are happy to throw in the towel when the going gets tough. I like to apply the same concept to meeting people. We already know it takes time, energy, and effort to meet people. For some of us that's exhausting, and for others, it's re-energizing. But how do you get from one side of the coin to the other? It all starts mentally.

If you tell yourself you're tired, exhausted, and that you just can't go out tonight because you don't have the energy, your wish will be granted. You have to dig deep, find that drive and get your butt out there. Being around other people is energizing because we all have our own energy and when you put that in one room of people, you can feel it when you walk in, which will help pick up your spirits.

WORDS OF CAUTION

Also, remember that having a spouse doesn't replace having a group of friends. I see this every week—people get in a relationship and then disappear from their group of friends, only to re-emerge when their relationship ends.

Here's some advice: **Your friends should like your boyfriend or girlfriend.** In a perfect world, your spouse should, at the very least, get along with your friends. I'm not saying that everyone needs to become best friends, but your friends need to approve of him or her, and your spouse needs to accept your friends. Your friends have known you longer than your significant other (in most scenarios), so why would you discount their opinion on who you're going out with? And even worse, why would you stop hanging out with them after you get in a relationship? There's enough time for both to co-exist, and if not, you're probably going out with the wrong person.

Trust your established friends; if they point out the flaws or character issues of someone you're dating, then you should seriously consider their viewpoints. If they're good friends, they should know you pretty well. Occasionally we get distracted by superficial features, but good friends will pull you aside and keep you in check—it's one reason why they're your friends! They keep you from doing stupid things. If you're hanging out with a questionable character, it's on them to remind you who you are and to question why you're with them.

TAKEAWAYS:

- Eliminate "I can't" and "I'm busy" from your vocabulary. Your words become your reality.

- Don't limit the number of friends you have—friends come in and out of our lives in cycles, so you need to keep the doors open to new people and new opportunities.

- Trust your good friends—sometimes they know you better than you know yourself.

Chapter 21

STEP EIGHTEEN: JUST BE...

BE PRESENT

Why worry about tomorrow when you have today? Live for today, with your friends, family, and all the good things around you. If you can focus on that, it will help immensely in meeting people. When you're out and about at events, be present, don't get distracted. Why do you think people have a hard time remembering people's names? Because they're not present. They're not paying attention. They hear the name but they don't absorb it.

In this era of distraction, being present is a challenge. How often do you go out to eat and see people texting on their phones, checking emails, or doing something other than what they're supposed to be doing? When you're at a restaurant you should be doing two things: eating, and enjoying the company of whomever you're with.

Be the guy or girl who lives in the present and gives your undivided attention to whoever you're with. People will appreciate you because of that and will respect you more than you can imagine. In the grand scheme of life, we are only here for so long, so why not live every moment as if it's your last? Live each day to the fullest, and be grateful. Be mindful of what's around you and soak it up.

BE ENGAGING

By being present you also force yourself to engage in the conversation. So many people go through the motions and can't recall anything from the conversation they were just in. What then is the point of even talking to those people, if you can't remember what you talked about? It's a waste of your time and their time. You have to focus, actively listen, ask the right questions and make an effort. If you don't want to be somewhere, then you shouldn't have gone. It's not fair to you and it's not fair to others if you have not prepared yourself to be present and to be engaged.

Before we had cell phones, Netflix, cable TV, and the internet, we had to be a participant in life and to talk to people, whether in person or a landline phone. In some respects, we need to go back to those days. It's just a matter of re-training your brain to get back to the basics of simple person to person conversations.

Who are the most popular people? Typically, great storytellers who get people to hang on every word they say. Of course, you don't necessarily have to be a great storyteller, but always have something great in your arsenal to share. Come prepared with some relevant, funny stories that will spark the interest of others and have them asking you questions. The stories have to be your stories, involve your life, and ideally, if you can make them relatable to the crowd you're talking to, you'll win over many people.

BE GENUINELY INTERESTED

When I worked in the staffing industry, I was effectively a salesman of people. It was my job to sell job candidates to the companies I was talking to. I was taught a variety of things while at that job, and one of the best things I took away was that you need to ask open-ended questions when talking to people, whether for business or for pleasure. From that point on, my conversations in and out of work completely changed. I made it my mission to stop asking yes or no questions, and instead to utilize the who, what, when, where, why, and how questions. When you do this it will be a game changer, because doing so makes you seem genuinely interested in the other person you're talking to. Secondarily, it typically forces people to answer questions on a deeper level.

BE HUMBLE

Having the right attitude is the key to getting started off on the right foot when entering a conversation, but there are also a few fine lines that need to be drawn as well. You must be humble. No one likes a braggart. This applies not only to what you say but what you do. I'm sure you see it every day on social media—people try to act tough, like more of a bad ass than they really are and to pretend that their life is 100% in order and everything is the best. But we all know that these are the misconceptions and traps of social media. People only post what they want you to see.

If you find yourself constantly taking selfies and posting them online, whether in the gym, your car, your bed, your office, or anywhere else—please stop. Actions speak louder than words or pictures, and people will have much more respect for you if you just stop with the selfies. Self-promotion will eventually work against you because people will think you're only into yourself.

BE FEARLESS

Do you remember the first day of school? Whether elementary, middle, high school or college, it doesn't really matter. Do you remember that feeling of uneasiness when you first walked through those doors and feel like people were looking at you and judging you based on what you were wearing, your hair color, your glasses, your skin color, or anything else? Well, if you can survive that, then guess what? You can walk into a room full of strangers and make friends as an adult!

Meeting people is not easy, especially when you're the new kid on the block or you are on your own at a party and everyone is in their own conversations. You look around, anxiously looking for someone you know, hoping they'll throw you a lifeline to get the conversation started. If that person never shows up, don't worry about it. Take a deep breath, and just go—walk up to someone or a group of people and confidently introduce yourself.

To be fearless do you have to be courageous? Not all the time. But to be fearless you do have to exude a certain amount of confidence. People who are fearless aren't afraid. They have a certain swagger when they walk, their tone of voice is strong, and their actions mimic their words. It's amazing what happens when you start saying "I can" or "I am." Those are strong, confident statements. "I can run a 5k in twenty-five minutes." "I am feeling great today." "I can do whatever I set my mind to." These statements set the tone for you and for the day. Try them out to see what happens. "Today, I am going to make new friends. I am going to walk into that room and have great conversations."

TAKEAWAYS:

- When you're with a friend, truly be with them. Don't be checking your phone.

- Have an arsenal of interesting stories ready to share when you go out.

- Be fearless. The hardest part is walking through the door.

Chapter 22

LEAVE A LEGACY

What will be your legacy? What will you accomplish that will make you proud? What will make you say, "Damn, I've lived one hell of a life?" Our lifetime is limited, but our impact goes far beyond what we think it can.

By writing this book, I hope to leave an impact on you. I want you to walk away from this book having learned more than a few things about how to meet and make friends, but also how to be inspired to live your life the way you want to live it. To live a life with meaning, with passion and purpose. I want you to wake up every day thinking about all the good things you're going to accomplish, how productive you're going to be, and how great it is to be alive.

Don't worry if you're unsure what you want your legacy to be. It's a journey, and it is not meant to be figured out right after college. That's the misnomer we've all been taught to believe. Right after college, you get a job, it becomes your career, and somehow people think it is what you should be doing the rest of your life. Don't get trapped in that box. It's your life, you can do whatever you want.

What do you strive for? What do you believe in? Who do you want to be? How do you want to be remembered? Every day you should have a goal of what you want to accomplish so that you can look back at the end of the day and reflect upon how successful you were. Of course, things always come up, we get busy, distracted, and things don't always work out the way we intended them to. But if you can say that you did the best that you could every single day, you're going to live a life that you can be proud of.

If things didn't go quite as you planned, remind yourself that tomorrow is a new day to make an impact. Don't worry about things outside of your control. Instead, give thanks at the end of each day. Whether you say it aloud or in your head, it doesn't really matter. Give thanks for being alive, for making new friends, and for everything that happened in the day that was good. Don't focus on the negative or anything that didn't work out in your favor. Be thankful for all the good and put 100% focus on that, as positive energy is what makes you happy and live a life that is fulfilled.

My friend Sing is a woman on a mission who will not let anything or anyone keep her from achieving her dreams. Her life has not been easy and through all the challenges she's faced, she's become a fighter, which has given her the drive to keep pushing when facing any new challenge. She now uses that drive to build her legacy by giving back to the community that has embraced her.

CASE STUDY: SING

I am the product of many blessings. It has taken countless miracles to get me to where I am in my life. When I was born in Vietnam, my mother lacked the nourishment to produce milk, so instead, I was fed rice water for the first few months. A year later, I was a toddler in my pregnant mother's arms when our escape boat began to take on water. As our family boarded a rescue vessel, we watched the small boat sink.

These and many more critical moments would continue to affect my life. I am grateful for our sponsorship to America, the loving church that took us in, and the government assistance that was given to help our family thrive. I also acknowledge the contributions of the many teachers and local community members who supported me and believed that I was worth their extra attention. I owe every accomplishment achieved to all of them.

It is because of these experiences that I can see myself in every young person I meet. I recognize their vulnerabilities and how easily their lives can be altered depending on the guidance they receive. As a restaurant owner with a large staff of millennials, it is my responsibility to encourage their growth and push them to achieve success in their lives. I am the product of the kindness of strangers and the concentrated efforts of those who believed in me. I do what I do because I know that I am not more deserving than anyone else. My blessings demand that I constantly contribute to the growth and development of future generations. I find joy in knowing that I will always have purpose in my life.

TAKEAWAYS:

- If you do your best every day, it's hard to have regrets.

- Give thanks daily.

- Don't let anything stop you from following your dreams and building your legacy.

Chapter 23

WRITE YOUR OWN DESTINY

"I am the captain of my ship, the master of my fate." This quote hangs above my desk on a plaque given to me by my dad before he passed away. He reminded me that in this life we live, it is up to us to carve our own path and create our own destiny. No one else dictates where you go in life—only you do.

So as a closing to this book, I want you always to remember that you control your own life. If you want friends, it is up to you to go out and seek them. Things don't magically fall in your lap. It takes grit and determination to make things happen, even the smallest things in life.

And don't worry about what others are up to. Sure, on the outside their lives may seem fun, easy, and carefree, but you don't know what it's like to walk in their shoes. People can smile all day long, but you have no idea what's hiding behind the smile. Maybe it's sincere, maybe it's just a front. The best way for you to move forward in life is to focus on you; have laser focus on your own life, and forget the rest.

What gifts do you have? How are you different than others? What makes you special? Think about those questions and how you can use those qualities while you write your own destiny. Many people overlook what they're really good at and miss the opportunity to leverage their best traits.

MAKE A ONE-YEAR PLAN

When you're thinking about your future, remember that things change every day. Having a "five-year plan" is really irrelevant. Don't get me wrong, it's nice to daydream and wonder about where you'll be in five years—perhaps who you're going to marry, where you're going to live, what job you will have, how much money you will have, and so on. But leave those questions to a psychic. There really is no way to know who you will meet tomorrow that could dramatically change your life.

Ask yourself this question: Where was I five years ago? What's your answer? Let me guess— you're in a place now that you would have never imagined, right? Probably because you happened to meet someone along the way who altered your life path during that time frame. That's why it's so very critical to go out, meet people, socialize, and network because every person you meet really does matter.

I would also like to note that your destiny is not written in stone; it's an unfinished book and you're the author of it. As I said before, the five-year plan is nothing more than a waste of time. Every five-year period I look back and think to myself, "Well, I didn't think I'd be doing what I'm doing today. Funny how life works out." So stop wasting time on making five-year plans and focus on the immediate future.

"Immediate" to me is having a solid one-year plan and at least an idea of what you want to accomplish in life. Life gets too complicated to plan any further out. You can't predict who you're going to meet tomorrow that is going to change your life one way or the other. The best you can do is be prepared for when you do come across that person—to have an idea of where you want to go.

MAKE IT HAPPEN

Your destiny is whatever you want it to be. If you want to be something, go out and be it. If you want to move somewhere, then pack up your bags and go. What are you waiting for? If you need a swift kick in the behind, then just ask me and I'll be happy to help out. Time waits for no one and the longer you wait, the more you'll regret your decisions. When opportunity knocks, what are you going to do? Stand on the sidelines and wait for the "perfect time" to make a decision, or jump into the game and see what happens? There never is a "right time"— there is only now.

If your passion is scuba diving and that's something you can see yourself doing for the rest of your life, then figure out a way to make that happen. If you're big into helping people out and doing charity work, then do that. You don't always have to quit your job to do what you love. It might just be a matter of making time to do what you love. Start small and maybe over time things will work themselves out to do what you love full-time.

In the end, I hope this book has given you useful information to get out there, to make friends, to spark a conversation, and to live the life you deserve. Use the power of positivity to make new friends and expand your horizons beyond your wildest dreams, for there are no limits in life. You can go as far as you want to.

Stay hungry my friends, for the adventure of a lifetime begins with one step off your couch and into the unknown.

TAKEAWAYS:

- You're the only one who has a direct impact on your life and the decisions you make everyday.

- Your destiny is not written in stone. It's an ever-changing, living document that you control.

- There are no limits in life. Dream big, love often, take risks, and never look back.

CONCLUSION

DO THE IMPOSSIBLE: TODAY IS THE DAY

What if you woke up and decided today is your day to do the impossible? No limits. No boundaries. What are you waiting for? You are only limited by the thoughts you place in your mind. This is your life and you can fly as high or as low as you choose.

You can also determine how many friends you want in your life. You can be a social butterfly, or you can keep it tight, with just a small circle of friends. Get out there and start somewhere. You don't have to attend three events per day, but start out with at least one event if not two per week.

Perhaps we've all been suckered into using mobile apps to meet people just because it's "easier" than meeting people in real life—the feeling of rejection isn't as high if you message someone via an app and they choose not to respond, right? But that's because we've also been taught to believe that it's the end of the world if we do get rejected. Trust me, it'll be ok. It's happened to me just like it's happened to you. Get over it, move on with life, and have the belief that there are better people out there for you to meet.

Making friends as an adult is not impossible—all it requires is taking that first step.

STEP UP TO THE PLATE

Going to a social event or networking group is like going up to face a pitcher in baseball. You're not going to hit 100 home runs out of 100 attempts. In fact, let's just talk hits. If you meet 100 people over a few months, maybe 20 to 30 of those will be good connections, or at least people you can do things with going forward. The rest? Well, you can't win them all, unfortunately, because in life we all have different personalities and different points of view. Some of us match, and some of us not so much. The trick is to go in with the mindset that it doesn't really matter what your batting percentage is. It's the fact that you're going up swinging. You're making an attempt to go out and meet people, and that is what going forward in life requires. It requires you to take that step up to the plate, to prepare yourself for the pitch, and swing.

But have the right mentality when you're stepping up to the plate—the belief that you are going to connect, that you are going to hit the ball and that you will be successful. So many times in life we tell ourselves, "Don't strikeout," "Don't look at a fastball," or don't do whatever. Instead, focus on all the good things to come. Envision who you want to be, and where you want to be in life, and use that vision to drive you forward. You truly are only limited to what your mind tells you, so open up and take that step to where you want to be.

Not to lay too heavy on sports analogies, but imagine you're the star basketball player on your old high school team. When you hit the basketball court, what is running through your head? Are you nervous? Excited? Do you have butterflies in your stomach? Do you feel the pressure? Good! You should—that means you're alive and you're just like the rest of us. In your life today, you need to treat each day as game day and get pumped up! It's time to go out and make new friends, and you can't go home with a big zero on the scoreboard.

Every time you leave the house and go to an event or party, you have to have the mentality that you're not going to walk away without talking to at least five new people, and hopefully making at least two solid connections. With a winning attitude and cheerful personality, those goals won't be any problem at all.

So what are you waiting for? Get out there and make things happen! Life is a game, and you're just a player. What moves will you make today?

To learn more about building friendships, improving your social skills, and meeting people, go to Andrew's website and sign up for his newsletter at andrewmachota.com. You can also follow him on Twitter @AndrewMachota.

If you're interested in starting a New Town Connections chapter in your city, send an email to info@newtownconnections.com and tell us more about you and your city!

AUTHOR BIO

Andrew Machota is the CEO and Founder of New Town Connections (NTC), which is an exclusive social club for young professionals in the Tampa Bay area. Previously he was a CPA and recruiter working in the finance and accounting field. After attending countless networking events as a recruiter from 2013 to 2014, he continued to hear the same story from people he met: "It's hard to make friends as an adult." He got to thinking about how he could address this challenge—one that he had faced as well—and the idea for New Town Connections came to him. He quit his job in 2015 to start the business and has never looked back.

The youngest of two children, Andrew was born to an entrepreneurial family. His father, Gene, ran his own sewer and septic business. From a very young age, Andrew worked for his dad, learning the ins and outs of running a business. When his father passed away in 2008, Andrew knew that he had to do something with his life to leave a legacy and to make his father proud.

Andrew's passion, purpose, and calling in life is to help people make friends through New Town Connections, and his goal is for the business to develop into a worldwide network.

CPSIA information can be obtained
at www.ICGtesting.com
Printed in the USA
LVOW07s1020100817
544504LV00001B/11/P